THE GOLDEN GUIDE TO

POWER BOATS

BILL WALLACE

GOLDEN HANDBOOK

LDEN PRESS, NEW YORK

PHOTO CREDITS:

Cover: Sante, Schwarm, Sheldon/Chris-Craft Corp.
Chris-Craft 28-foot Constellation
cruiser and MFG's 16½-foot runabout, the Edinboro,
powered by a 40-hp Johnson outboard.

Chris-Craft Corp.: Page 18.

Evinrude: Pages 16-17 (No. 3), 51, 60, 67 (top), 84, 115, 131 (top), 140-141, 144, 160.
Johnson Motors: Pages 8 (top, middle), 12, 16-17 (Nos. 1, 7), 17 (right), 25, 42 (top), 54, 55, 61, 66, 67 (bottom), 68, 77, 81, 87, 93, 103, 112-113, 116, 125, 150, 151 (top right & left).
James Kavallines: Page 123.
McCulloch Corp.: Pages 16-17 (Nos. 2, 6), 17 (bottom), 19, 42 (bottom), 95 (top), 142, 143, 146, 151 (middle row & bottom).
Mercury Outboard Motors: Pages 4, 6, 8 (bottom), 9, 10, 16-17 (Nos. 4, 5), 22, 24 (top left & right), 28, 34, 35, 36, 48, 63, 69, 73 (bottom), 86, 89, 90-91, 92 (bottom), 95 (bottom), 108-109, 117, 119 (bottom), 120, 148 (bottom).
Norwalk Boat Works: Pages 10-11.
Outboard Boating Club of America: Page 99.
Owens-Corning Fiberglas: Page 155.
Raytheon Corp.: Pages 70, 73 (top).
Morris Rosenfeld: Pages 14-15, 24 (bottom), 26, 27, 32-33, 45, 46, 52, 64-65, 76, 78, 79, 92 (top), 96, 105, 106-107, 110-111, 122, 129 (bottom), 136-137, 138, 145, 153, 154, 156, 157.
U.S. Coast Guard: Page 114.

 Designed and produced by The Ridge Press, Inc. Printed in the U.S.A. by Western Printing and Lithographing Company. Published by Golden Press, Inc., 850 Third Avenue, New York, New York · Published simultaneously in Canada by The Musson Book Company, Ltd., Toronto.

CONTENTS

1

POWERBOATING: PLEASURE & CHALLENGE

The pleasures and challenges of life on the water have been known generally to people for centuries. But they have taken on new meaning in recent years for millions of Americans for whom boating has become a leading recreational sport. This book is about both of these elements of life afloat, but it is somewhat more concerned with mastering the challenges as a means of guaranteeing the pleasures. For boating demands that a number of skills be acquired to make the craft behave properly under normal conditions, and that quick and accurate responses be ingrained for emergency use in time of danger.

ANATOMY OF A BOAT

A boat takes a lot of knowing. Its capabilities and limitations should be completely familiar before one ventures to take command. And the learning process should be viewed as a continuing thing. Not even the oldest salt claims to know everything about boats and boating. The way to learn is to listen, to watch, to read, and to remember. Delightful days spent on the water will make the effort to learn more than worthwhile.

Learning begins with an understanding of the language of boating, the many terms that seem so foreign at first, but rapidly become a part of the boatman's vocabulary. And with reason, for correct terminology is essential to clear communication between skipper and crew. Compare terms below with picture opposite.

BOW: Forward part of the boat.
STERN: Area in rear of the boat.
FORWARD: Going toward the bow, the bow area.
AFT: Going toward the stern, the stern area.
PORT: The left side of the boat when facing forward.
STARBOARD: Right side when facing forward.
BEAM: Width of the boat from one side to the other.
HULL: Body or shell of boat.
WATERLINE: Line where the surface of the water touches the hull when the boat is at rest.
FREEBOARD: Distance from waterline to top of boat.
GUNWALE: The top edge all around the hull.
CHINE: Lower edge of the hull where bottom, sides join.
TRANSOM: The back of the boat across the stern.
HATCH: The cover over an opening in the deck.
CLEAT: Metal casting on deck to secure ropes.
CHOCK: A fitting through which the deck lines lead.

Boats come in many shapes and sizes for a variety of purposes. Fun on the water can mean a cookout on a houseboat (left), a joy ride with a fiberglass outboard cruiser (below), a family voyage aboard a pontoon craft (bottom), or a speedy trip to a quiet beach in a twin-hulled outboard catamaran

POWERBOATING: PLEASURE & CHALLENGE

A moving boat is said to be underway. Power may come from an outboard motor attached to the transom outside the hull, or from an inboard engine secured to the inner hull and covered by the deck or an engine hatch. Power is transmitted to the bladed propeller under the stern to move the hull forward. Except for the smallest outboards, modern boats have forward and reverse gears operated by a shift lever located next to the helmsman's seat. Boats have no brakes, but they will back up—or, more correctly, "back down."

An outboard is steered by turning the entire motor. Inboards steer by rudders set under the stern.

This Norwalk cruiser is all set to go. But some knowledge is needed about how to make it go

When a rudder is turned one way, water pushes against it, sending the stern scooting the other way. When the stern moves to the right, the bow will go to the left. The bow's direction is thereby controlled by the stern: left rudder, left turn; right rudder, right turn.

To get into a boat is to come aboard—and with small craft some care is required. Step into the middle of a small boat, not on the gunwale, because a lot of weight there will cause the hull to tip suddenly and perhaps drastically. Never step aboard with a load of gear. Put the gear down on the dock or float, and load it after having safely boarded the boat.

2

HOW TO BUY A BOAT

The first step in buying a boat is to determine how it will be used. There are hundreds of different kinds of boats. Some are ideal for one activity, some for another, and some are versatile enough to serve several purposes. The most successful purchase, therefore, is the one that matches the best capabilities of the craft with the intentions of the owner. Cost is a consideration, certainly. Few people have unlimited funds to spend on boating. But cost alone is not necessarily a reliable guide to a satisfactory boat. Chris-Craft, the country's largest boatbuilder, has a 66-foot model that sells, fully equipped, for almost $166,000. On the other hand, the lowest priced boat exhibited at a recent New York motorboat show was a flat-bottom

dinghy made of sheet plywood and costing $85. The 66-footer would be fine for a cruise from New York to Chicago, but hardly practical for a fishing expedition to a gunk hole. The dinghy, which can float in a few inches of water, would be a dandy fishing boat and totally inadequate for an extended trip.

Most boats are bought for fishing, cruising, or water skiing. Even here, however, requirements should be carefully defined. Fishing boats range from the $85 dinghy or a $100 rowboat, ideal for perch fishing at anchor, to $50,000, 40-foot cruisers designed for deep-sea fishing. What is your pleasure? Modern 12- to 16-footers are perfect for small game fish. Many offer good stowage space for extra fuel tanks, bait boxes, anchors, and other gear. The newer outboard motors offer power and speed enough to get the fisherman

A rafting party finds a dozen cruisers secured in a quiet cove at the end of the day. The visiting hour is at hand

where he wants to go without delay, yet can be throttled down for the slowest kind of trolling. Cruising also imposes choice. It can mean a Sunday afternoon joy ride, an overnight camping trip, or—with sleep-aboard boats—a complete family vacation.

The fastest-growing boating activity is water skiing. Originally expensive and requiring an inboard runabout, skiing has been brought within the reach of modest pocketbooks by the development of more powerful outboard engines. It is possible to ski behind any boat that can reach 20 miles per hour. The only prerequisite is the ability to swim—which applies to every phase of boating.

Finally, for the specialists there are boats suitable for skin diving, different types of racing, predicted-log cruiser competition, and even commuting. For many

1

2

4

What to do with a boat? There exists a wide choice of water-borne activities to suit different tastes and pocketbooks. A boat is a vehicle for adventure. The choices, each requiring its own equipment and special skills, include working the inshore fishing holes with an outboard (1 & 7); camping overnight on an island (2); teaching a youngster how to water ski (3); marathon racing in the open sea (4); enjoying a scenic, daytime cruise (5); going below with an aqualung for a look at the bottom (6). Take your pick

5

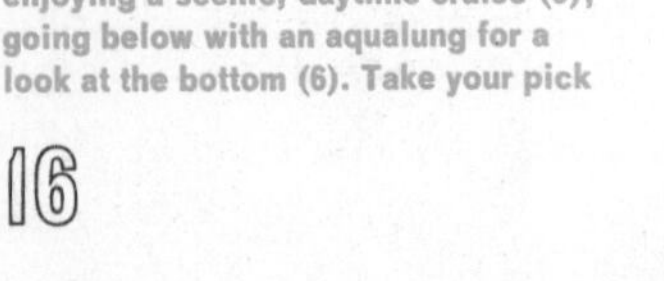

3

6

7

mariners, acquiring a boat may mean buying a trailer, as well. This is an added expense, but it also has many advantages. For one thing, it enables the boatowner to keep his craft at home, where it is not only safe but conveniently at hand for upkeep and repair. In the more populous areas, the trailer also solves the growing problem of overcrowded anchorages and docking facilities, and saves the cost of mooring and maintenance fees.

In fact, the efficient, reliable boat trailer has made a major contribution to the boating boom of the past decade. Prior to World War II, the boating enthusiast was largely confined to his home waters and the sport was beyond the reach of those living far from a shore-

Tiedown strap secures the craft (far left) to its trailer. Left: The smaller outboard burns less fuel for fishermen when trolling; bigger ones are for speed

line. Today the trailer makes boating possible even for families living hundreds of miles inland. It also makes boatowners mobile. They can trail their craft to a variety of waterways anywhere in the country.

Trailers now are available that can tow boats ranging from small fishing skiffs to 25-foot family cruisers behind the family car. Trailers cost from $150 to $1,500, depending on size, load-bearing capacity, and such extra features as electric winches, hydraulic lifts, and independent brakes.

Driving tips: Brake sooner, accelerate and drive more slowly, make wide swings on corners, and allow plenty of room when passing. Also, halt frequently to check the load for slippage or stresses.

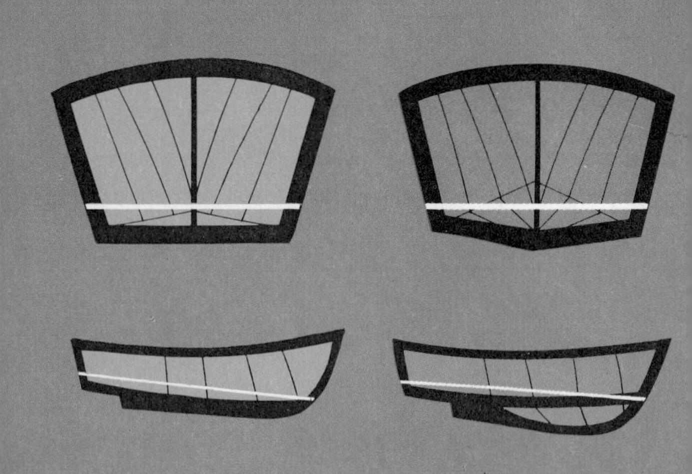

Riding qualities are determined by hull forms. Basic types ar

Boat hulls come in three basic forms: flat-bottom, round-bottom, and V-bottom. Each has its advantages and limitations. The flat-bottom hull is the least expensive to build, but the least stable to operate. It is suitable only for protected waters and found mostly in small rowboats or fishing outboards. The round-bottom design, an old concept, is long on comfort and seaworthiness, but expensive to construct. The efficient compromise is the V-bottom, which combines stability with building simplicity. It gives maximum interior space without too great a loss of comfort. This form is common among outboard runabouts and small cruisers.

HULL FORMS

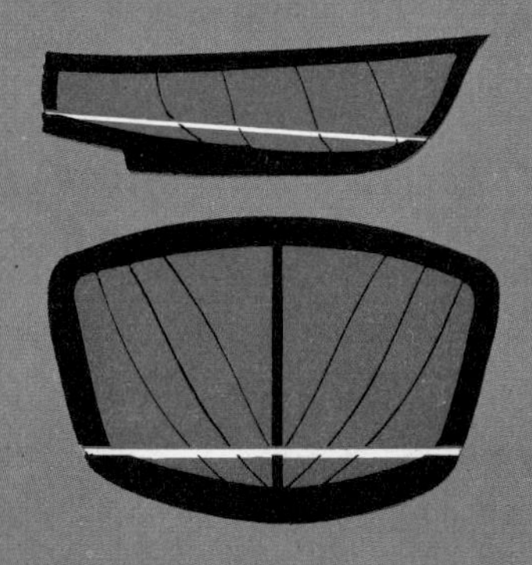

lat-bottom (left), V-bottom (middle), round-bottom (right)

Large, heavy craft are generally called displacement hulls. This means they displace water as they move through it. Smaller boats, especially outboards, are generally planing craft. At speed, they move over the water rather than through it. Displacement hulls, therefore, are slower than planing boats, but they provide more riding comfort and stability in rough water. Planing hulls have a disadvantage in that they are difficult to handle at non-planing speeds (roughly, under 15 miles per hour). These boats are distinguished by wide, flat stern sections. Some of the more refined designs manage to combine the round and V-bottom

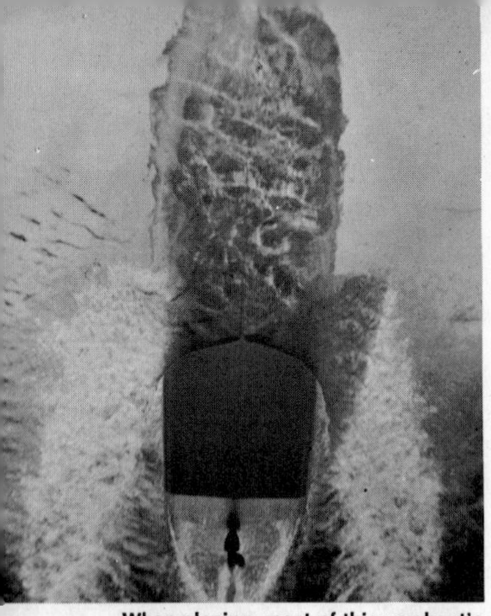

When planing, most of this runabout's hull rides free of the water

characteristics. For example, there are larger hulls with round or V-sections forward and flat planing sections leading aft. These boats, with sizeable power plants, are capable of planing at high speeds at no great loss of comfort for the passengers.

Another variation in hull form is in the draft—how deep into the water the hull will ride. Deep-draft hulls, whether round or V-bottom, assure stability at a sacrifice of speed, while shallow-draft vessels have opposite characteristics. As for materials, hulls today are made of wood, fiberglass (a reinforced plastic), aluminum, and occasionally steel. Wooden boats are of many different types, utilizing conventional planking, lapstrake or clinker-built planking, sheet plywood, or molded plywood. Planked boats require an elaborate

This molded plywood hull has round chines, flat-bottom aft and V-bottom forward

inner skeleton of frames, ribs, stem, and keel fastened with screws, nails, or rivets. Lapstrake models, using the round-bottom hull, overlap their planks like the clapboard siding of a house. This lapping adds strength and stability to the underbody of the boat, as the laps act as a check against the rolling of the hull.

Among boats of 20 feet or under, fiberglass has made immense gains within the past five years. This material, consisting of glass fibers and hard, glue-like resins, is ideal for the molding of all kinds of boat shapes, and the more curves the better. Fiberglass boats are very durable. They do not leak and require painting less frequently than wooden ones. Aluminum boats offer light weight and strength; sheet plywood offers low cost; molded plywood, durability and no leaking.

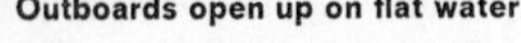
Outboards open up on flat water

Beaching a flat-bottom craft

Luxury cruiser by Wheeler even has radar set for navigational aid

Twin-engined outboard cruiser is equipped for deepwater fishing

MATCHING BOAT & MOTOR

Which boat will it be: model A, B, or C? Choosing the right boat means knowing how it will be used—whether for cruising, fishing, water skiing, or a little of all three. A second consideration is the character of the available water. A boat suitable for a shallow river would be all but useless on exposed coastal waters. A natural third factor is how much to spend. A sensible start for a beginner would be with a small, simple boat. If fishing is the primary interest, a good choice is a 12- to 14-foot open craft of modified flat-bottom design—a vessel that hopefully would never be expected to do combat with four-foot waves. For power, an outboard

motor of 18 horsepower or less is recommended. Twelve-foot boats are adequate, but those under 10 feet are usually designed for special purposes and have a tendency to tip over easily.

The more ambitious the fishing, the larger the boat should be. For open-water trips, a 16- to 18-foot runabout is best—one with plenty of beam, a decked-over bow, high windshield, convertible top, and a husky motor of at least 25 horsepower. Larger fishing boats will be inboard powered, which means a big jump in price and weight, but a resulting savings in fuel. Two-cycle outboards from 60 to 80 horsepower are notorious for their avid fuel thirst, a habit the four-cycle inboards lack.

Good cruising boats need plenty of room for stowage. An overnight cruise is entirely possible in outboard runabouts as small as 14 or 16 feet. Boats the manufacturers call outboard cruisers begin at the latter length. These are cramped compromises, however. A

Fishing chairs (left) in spacious cockpit of 42-foot Martinique Cruiser by Matthews (below)

feasible cruiser with a pair of honest sleeping berths is going to be 18 feet long or more. Add a galley, a marine toilet (called a head), a dinette, and two more berths and our cruiser is now at least a 26-footer costing $8,000.

Speeds of 20 miles per hour and up are the fundamental requirement of a water-ski boat. Others would be a well-mounted towing ring, good forward and aft visibility for the driver and observer, reasonable ease in climbing aboard, and space for skis and fuel tanks. Outboards of 14 to 18 feet fill the bill, inboards of 16 to 20 feet. The more skiers to tow the more power is needed.

Are there boats so versatile they can do everything—cruise, fish, and ski? Yes, but they may be compromises. The best kind would be a husky 18-foot outboard runabout with a planing hull, a big motor of over 50 horsepower for speed, and cockpit space galore for berths and stowage.

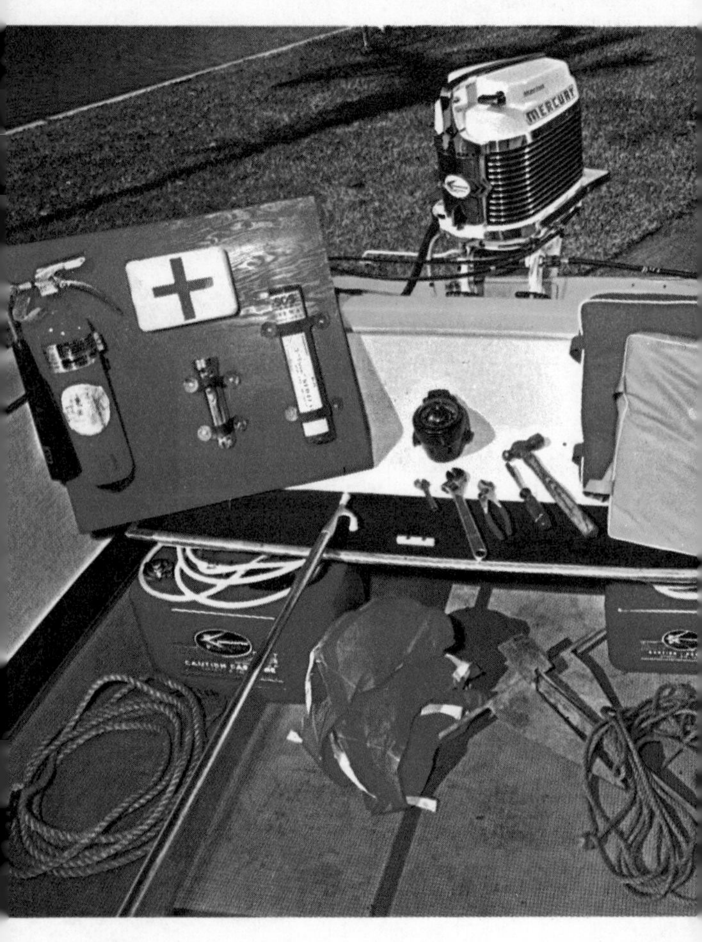
MERCURY

BASIC EQUIPMENT

Equipping a boat from scratch can be one of the most pleasant—and expensive—experiences in the sport. Because of the many gadgets and accessories on the market, the new boatowner may feel that he is obligated to furnish a house afloat. Not so. There are essential equipment items for every boat, many of them required by law, but a ship on a tight budget can do without a lot of the extras. The number of items required varies with the size of the boat and the purposes to which it will be put. Use a check list, like the one that follows, as a guide.

ESSENTIAL

Navigational Lights: See Chapter 6 for requirements stated in Federal and state laws.

Fire Extinguisher: See Chapter 6 for requirements.

Life Jackets: Have enough to equal the maximum number of passengers. Approved cushions may be substituted.

Pump: Lightweight plastic ones are best and require an extension that will carry the water overboard.

Tool Kit: It should include pliers, screwdriver, spare spark plugs, waterproof tape, wrenches, rope, and knife.

Anchor: See Chapter 3 for recommended types and sizes.

Lights: A search- or flashlight, complete with extra batteries, is a must on all boats.

Paddle: Necessary, "just in case," on small boats.

This well-supplied helmsman has within reach (left to right) radio, binoculars, clock, mirror, barometer, tachometer, compass, choke, starter key, fire extinguisher

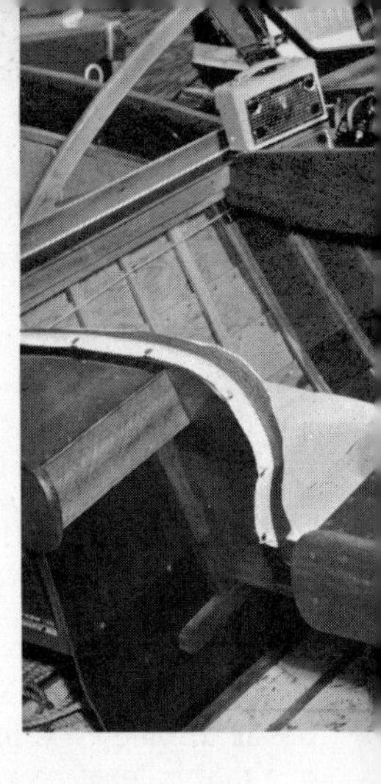

BASIC EQUIPMENT

Compass: Always a handy item, essential for navigation in strange waters or poor visibility.

Bucket and Sponge: Most-used equipment aboard, these items keep deck, bilges, and cockpit clean.

Whistle or Horn: See Chapter 6 for requirements.

Deck Lines: For securing boat fore and aft, also for spring lines, anchoring, towing, skiing.

Fenders: Of rubber or plastic, these protect the finish of the topsides when docking or tying to others.

First Aid Kit: Should be complete enough to handle minor emergencies, and in a waterproof case.

Speedometer: Valuable as a means of checking engine performance and also to curb speeds in harbors.

Resusitube: This plastic tube, costing $1.50, is recommended for administering artificial respiration.

Spare Fuel Tank: It should be filled, too. Running out of gas in a boat is inexcusable—and can be disastrous.

NON-ESSENTIAL

Rear Vision Mirror: A handy gadget for water-ski drivers and others who need 360-degree visibility.
Foul Weather Gear: Guests will appreciate waterproof jackets and pants when weather turns bad.
Binoculars: Handy for spotting landmarks and buoys.
Spare Propeller: Nice to have aboard in case of an accidental grounding.
Portable Radio: Good for obtaining weather reports.
Electronics: Radio direction finders, Fathometers, ship-to-shore transmitters and Citizens' Band radios are built for boats as small as outboard runabouts. Larger inboards often have radar, loran, and television sets.
Boat Hook: For picking up moorings, fending off piers.
Engine Alarm Systems: Will indicate presence of gas fumes in bilge and resulting danger of explosion.
Flags: They are a part of traditional boating etiquette.

WHERE TO KEEP THE BOAT

Boating is beset with a parking problem. Finding a place to moor is becoming evermore difficult as the boating population soars. There are three possibilities: a mooring, a slip, or a trailer. (A mooring is a float or buoy connected by rope or chain to a permanent anchor on the bottom. A slip is an individual stall formed by floats or pilings set out from a pier.) A slip in a modern marina is ideal, if you can get one. In addition to protection, a marina offers all the services a boatowner could want: maintenance and repair, winter storage, fuel, ice, water, dockside power, a restaurant, motel, supply store, and perhaps a swimming pool. Slips cost $3 per foot and up for the season. At the new

Bahia Mar Marina
at Fort Lauderdale, Fla., has
slips for 400 boats

dry-land marinas for outboards, boats are stored on racks and can be lifted in or out of the water by a fork lift on short notice.

In many areas, boat or yacht clubs provide slip or mooring privileges along with membership. Dues at these clubs may be as little as $5 a year or as much as $500. Certain areas are designated as public anchorages and minimum fees are charged here. Boat-owners can obtain moorings by application to the town harbor master, provided vacancies exist. It's a rare harbor that has more moorings than boats.

For many, the solution is to keep the boat at home on a trailer. Loading and launching a boat every time it is used can be a nuisance, but home storage is the best protection against the problems of storm damage, theft, or vandalism.

The best friend of the trailer sailor is a convenient, gently graded launching ramp close to deep water. There are not enough of these facilities in our country at the present time, particularly on the ocean coasts where the rise and fall of tidal waters make ramps difficult and expensive to install. Ramps may be municipally or privately owned and usually charge a dollar or so to launch and retrieve a boat. Beware of ramps that are too steep or have slippery surfaces. The best coverings are asphalt, cement, or crushed rock. Sand beaches, no matter how hard they may appear, are

Dry-land marina stores customers' boats in racks

Take the boat home on a trailer

dangerous. A car's wheels can easily sink or dig in and entrap the entire rig. Also avoid places where no one has launched before.

If a boat's home is to be a trailer, the two components had best match one another. Every trailer has a maximum load. In calculating it, remember that it includes the hull, the motor, and all the gear. An overloaded trailer is hard to tow and prone to flat tires and broken springs. The boat's weight should be well-balanced and secured by tie-down straps. The trailer hitch on the stern of the car should be welded to the frame, not merely bolted to the bumper. If the total weight (trailer, boat, motor, gear) exceeds one ton, the trailer should have its own set of brakes operating in conjunction with the car brakes. Trailers must be carefully maintained. Guard against rust formations.

MAKING FAST TO CLEAT

SHEET BEND

B

C

A

D

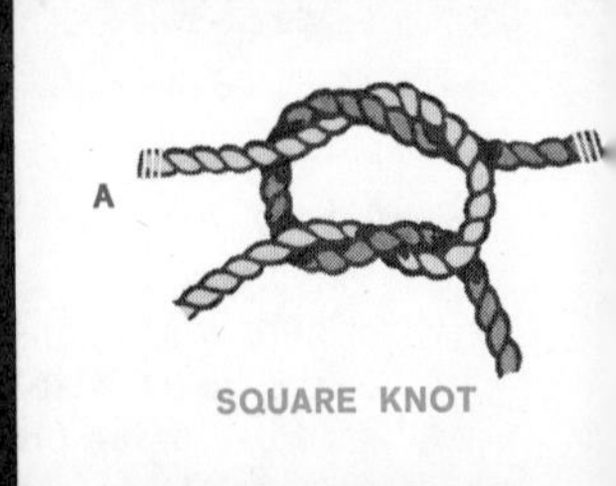

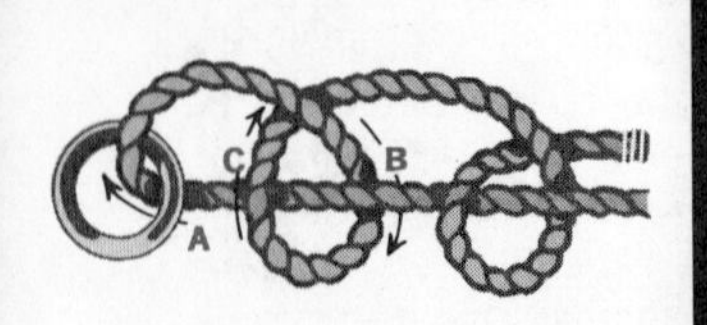

TWO HALF HITCHES

3

DECK SEAMANSHIP

Since a loose line could mean the loss of a boat, every sailor must be able to tie a few basic knots quickly and correctly. The clove hitch is a quick and reliable means to secure a line to a piling on a dock. The way to tie it is to make a loop in the line and drop the loop over the piling. Then make a second loop, with the running end on the underside of the loop, drop that over the piling and pull everything tight. The running end (or bight) is that section of the line used in the knot itself, while the standing part means the section that secures the boat to the dock. The only objection to the clove hitch comes when great strains are set upon a line and the hitch is pulled so tight that it becomes difficult to free in a hurry.

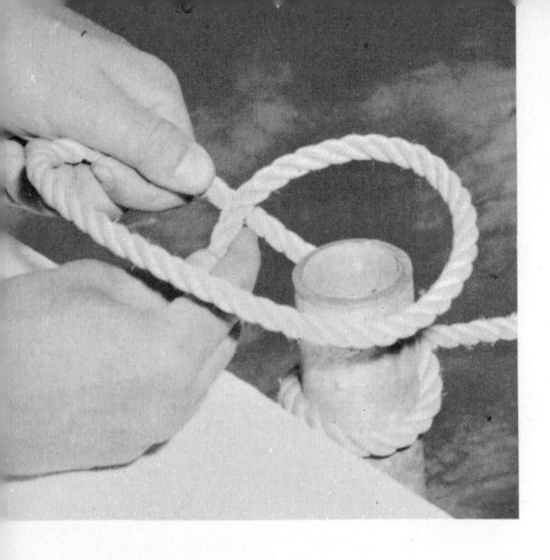

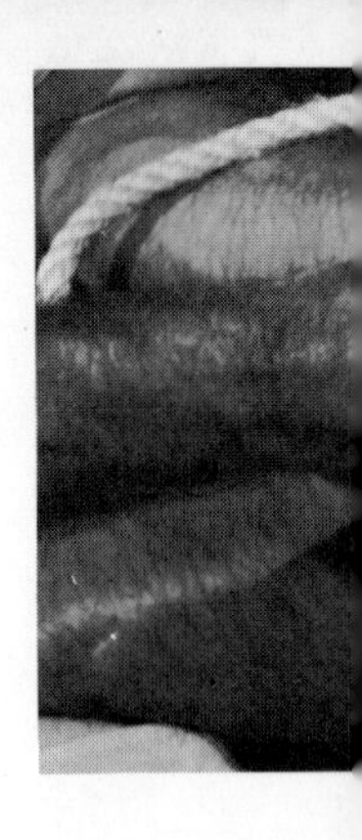

The reef or square knot is used in joining two pieces of rope. The knot is tied (see page 36) by passing (A) over and under (B). Then form a loop with (A). Pass (B) around the back of the loop and then through it. Pull the ends tight and make sure the end of the line and the standing part come out of the loop on the same side. If they are on opposite sides, it will be a "granny" knot which may slip, or jam so it cannot be untied.

The bowline is a knot that will neither slip nor jam. It can be used as a sling, a safety belt, or when an eye is needed in the end of the rope (see page 36). Make a loop (A) in the standing part of the line. Pass the end (B) up through the loop, around the back of the standing part (C), then return it down through the loop and draw it tight. Practice ashore with a short piece. The easiest way to secure the end of a line to another

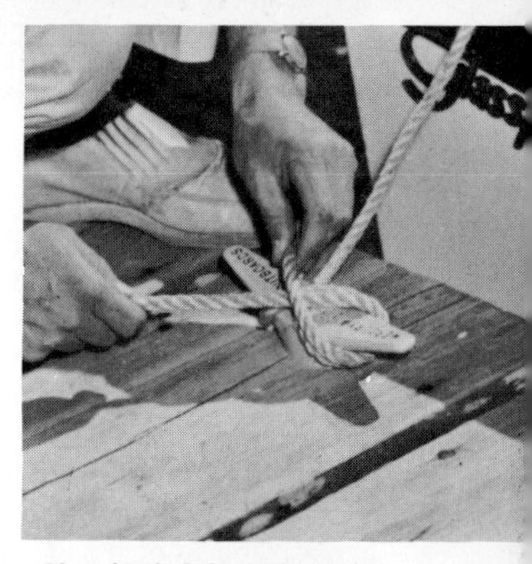
Clove hitch (left) made over a post won't slip. Splicing (center) joins two ropes permanently. When making fast to a dock cleat (right), use a half hitch and a turn

object, such as a piling or a mooring eye, is with the half hitch. Two half hitches will make the knot stronger. The drawing on page 36 shows the rope passing through the eye (A). Then it goes under and around the standing part (B and C). Repeat the turns to make two hitches.

The sheet bend is used to join two ropes of unequal sizes. Make a loop in the end of the larger line (as shown on page 36). Pass the end of the smaller rope through the loop (A), around in back (B), then in front (C), and under its own standing part (D).

There are several other knots but these will do for the learning boatman. Generally, a bend means a knot that unites two rope ends, while a hitch secures a rope to another object, such as a cleat. For greater strength, splicing is used to join two ropes.

ANCHORS & ANCHORING

A proper anchor and anchor line (called a rode) are the best insurance a boatowner can have. An anchor must have plenty of length of line (scope) to do a good job. How long? At least five times the depth of the water for effective holding and also to make the pull on the line more horizontal than vertical. A short length of chain between anchor and rode will keep the anchor lying flat to the bottom and therefore holding in its best position. For boats up to 20 feet long, anchor line is of manila or nylon, 3/8- or 1/2-inch thick and about 100 feet long. Add 25 feet more for 25-to-30-foot boats, and use 150 feet on those in the 30-to-40-foot class. Store anchor in an easily accessible place.

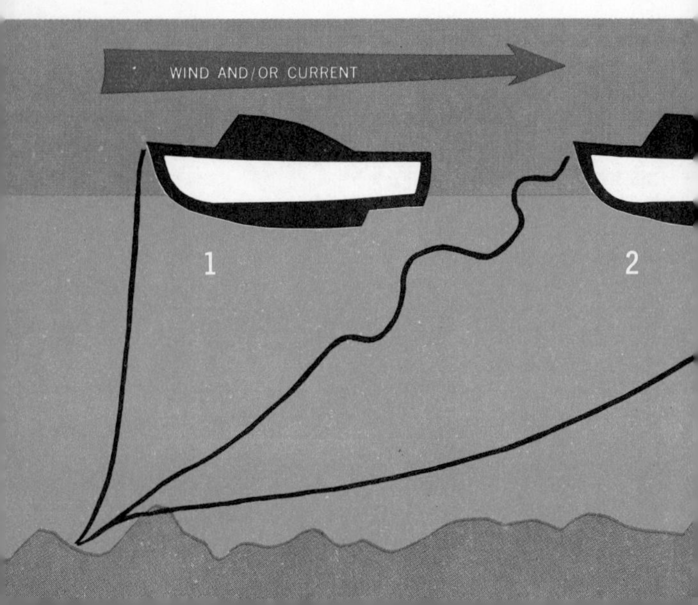

There are several different kinds of anchors, but the three types that best suit powerboats are the yachtsman's, the mushroom, and the patent models. The yachtsman's anchor is a traditional type—heavy, clumsy to store on smaller boats, vulnerable to fouling its own line. But when set firmly in the bottom it is as effective as any holding device can be. The simple mushroom has two uses: as a permanent holding anchor for a mooring or, in a lightweight size, as a temporary grip. But for reliable holding against ravages of wind and sea, even a small outboard boat deserves a patent anchor, such as a Danforth or a Northill. These are light, fold to stow, and quickly dig into the bottom.

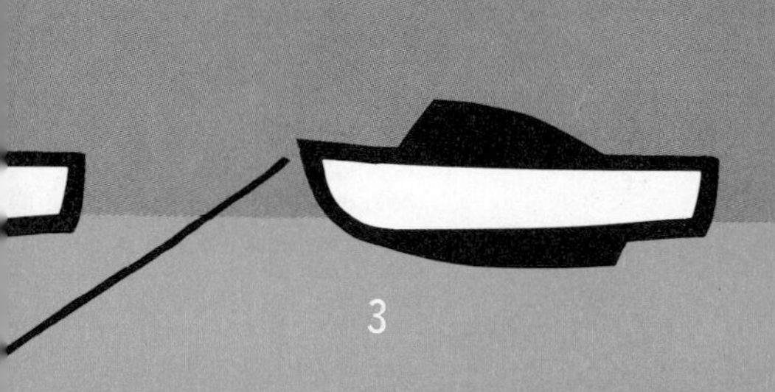

Boat comes to stop as anchor goes overboard (1), then sags back while line runs out (2). Reverse engines to set anchor (3)

Heaving anchor with twisted line is wrong

Anchor is dropped overboard at a stopover anchoring site

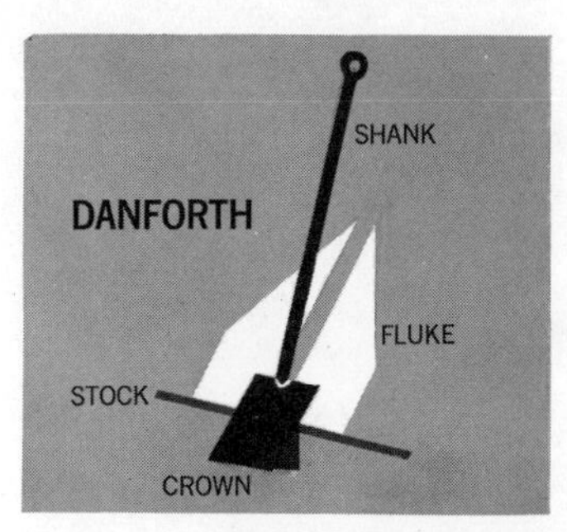

Light, patent-type anchor

ANCHORS & ANCHORING

A good solution for powerboats 18 feet long or more is to carry two holding devices—the small mushroom or "lunch" anchor plus the more muscular patent type. The important parts of the anchor are the stock, the shank, and the flukes. The Danforth's broad flukes really dig into the bottom. The manufacturer claims that the harder the pull, the deeper the anchor will work. An eight-pounder is recommended for craft of up to 16 feet, a 13-pounder for those 16 to 20 feet, a 22-pounder for boats 20 to 40 feet long. The best kinds of holding ground are sticky mud or clay, sand, or gravel. Soft mud and rocky bottoms make poor areas for anchoring.

To drop an anchor one does not throw it out enthusiastically as though casting for fish. The best way is to head the boat into the wind or current and bring the boat to a stop. Then gently lower the anchor over the side, paying out the line until it goes slack, indicating the hook is on the bottom. Then back the boat down slowly, permitting the flukes to dig in and hold.

DECK LINES

There are three types of deck lines that concern skippers of small boats. These are the bow line, stern line, and two spring lines. The first two secure the craft's bow and stern, while the spring lines keep the boat from moving forward or backward when alongside a dock. These lines have to be long enough to handle any docking situation the boat might encounter. Their length, even for a 16-foot runabout, should be at least 15 feet. Each line should have an eye splice that will fit comfortably over the bow or stern cleats. In many docking situations, particularly those of short duration,

Tying up, bow and stern, in a crowded marina brings confusing maze of lines, lines, lines

bow and stern lines will suffice when secured with bowline or clove hitch. For longer periods and in situations where the water is running swiftly, spring lines are needed. The stern spring line leads from the stern cleat of the boat forward to the piling or cleat on the dock. The bow spring line is led from the bow cleat aft to the dock. When mooring a boat in a slip, bow and stern lines on both port and starboard sides will keep the craft in position. In tidal conditions, it is essential to leave slack in the lines for the rise and fall of the water.

FUELING

The preparation of a boat for fueling should never be a haphazard business, but rather one of the more carefully executed operations. Gasoline explodes and so do boats with careless cigarette smokers aboard. Precautions are essential. This is especially true of inboards because of the easy build-up of volatile gasoline vapors in nonventilated areas such as bilges. The answer is to ventilate the hull thoroughly by using air vents on solidly installed fuel tanks, plus a blower fan in the bilges. Smoking should be forbidden. During the actual fueling, the nozzle of the hose should be

Utmost care is required on and around gas docks, when preparing fuel for an outboard, or filling the tanks of a power cruiser

thoroughly grounded to the fill opening, thus avoiding the possibility of a static spark causing an explosion. Spilled fuel must be cleaned up, and when the operation is concluded the boat should be ventilated for a few minutes with engine hatches open.

Since the outboard's fuel tanks are generally out in the open, there is less hazard when fueling. However, it is wise to take all the precautions used on an inboard. The best fueling stations are those that have a pump easily accessible on the end of a dock. The dock should be protected from rough water.

4

BOAT HANDLING

It has been said that anyone who can drive a car can drive a boat. While this may be true, it is an oversimplification. Many more factors work on a boat than on a car: weather, rough water, tide and current, fuel capacity, hull design. So, good seamanship requires special knowledge and experience, and the ability to apply them. Even as a motorist learns to cope automatically with a traffic situation, so should the boatman learn to cope—but with a much greater number of situations. For example: How to pass through a lock like the one in the picture opposite. The skipper must know his boat as he knows his wife—its strengths and its limitations. He must know the laws and the rules of the road. Finally—the subject of this chapter—he must know the techniques of boat handling.

To clear a dock, use a spring line (A). Turn the motor away from pier and go forward, swinging stern out. Reverse into open water (B), then pull away (C)

LEAVING THE DOCK

The new boatowner might assume he leaves a dock in the same way his auto leaves the curb—merely turn the wheel and move out. The same method applied to a boat could seriously damage the craft. A car has a pivot point at the rear wheels, while that of a boat is near its middle, forward of amidships. Thus, the boat turned quickly at a dock will have its stern raked and bumped along the pilings before it clears. The way to leave a dock is to cast off the lines and move almost straight ahead, barely turning the bow away from shore. Within a length or two, the hull will clear the dock and a hard turn can be made.

However, there may not be enough room. To leave a crowded dock, turn the wheel all the way to the open water. Then, with bow line secured to the dock, go forward slowly. The stern will turn away from the dock. As soon as the stern has cleared, the bow line can be cast off. Next, the wheel is turned to the center, the motor reversed, backing into open water. The motor is then put in forward gear and the helmsman can clear the dock and other boats. This technique applies equally to outboards, with all-in-one lower units (steering and propeller), and inboards. However, the latter have rudders placed behind the propellers and their reactions are somewhat slower. The "feel" is different. Make allowances.

A

B

C

UNDERWAY

The first outing in a new or unfamiliar boat should be on calm, protected waters. The idea is to find out just what the craft can and cannot do. How much distance does it take to slow down from high speed to idle? (A planing outboard hull slows quickly once it breaks its planing action.) How much room does the boat need to turn a complete circle with comfort? How quick is the response to a turn of the wheel? After a few introductory runs, the helmsman learns the feel of his boat and its handling becomes simple and a delight.

When underway, all powerboats throw up a wake which can cause discomfort or damage to others. Always be conscious of your boat's wake, especially close to shore

The next step is to learn a boat's handling characteristics under difficult water conditions, such as crossing the wake of another craft or running in rough water. Small boats taking wakes or waves head-on will be pounded unmercifully. To cross a wake line smoothly, for instance, it should be approached at an angle of about 45 degrees. Similarly, rough water should be taken with the bow at a slight angle. Running into a sea is wet, sloppy going, but seldom dangerous if speed has been reduced to avoid strain on the boat and its occupants. Running in the trough (valley between the waves) is no joy with wind and seas attacking on the beam. The helmsman should meet the largest of the seas by quartering into the wave momentarily—that is, by turning the bow into the wave, then straightening out to run down the valley that follows a heavy sea.

The most dangerous course of all is running before the waves. The boat is lifted by the stern and all control may be lost if the rudder and propeller break clear of the water. Then the boat will broach to—lie broadside in the trough—where it can be boarded by the following wave or even rolled over. Broaching can be avoided by careful, controlled steering under a slow throttle. Weight should be concentrated aft to keep the stern down. In extremely rough water there is nothing to do but heave to. This means heading into the waves at a slight angle with power reduced so the boat has steerageway but not headway.

Approach a dock (below) in slow forward speed, angling into wind or current. For the final few feet, shift into neutral gear. When the boat is opposite the landing space (right), the engine is turned away from the dock and into reverse. Reversing will bring the boat into the dock

COMING TO DOCK

Approaching a dock usually should be done from a shallow angle. Lines must be ready in both bow and stern, and bumpers in place to prevent scratching the topsides. Docking is accomplished at slow speed. If all goes well the motor can be shifted to neutral about a boat length from the dock. The boat can then drift up to the dock bow first and be brought broadside by turning the wheel toward the dock and briefly putting the engine in reverse. Whenever possible a boat should dock with the bow heading into the wind or current. If approaching the weather side of a dock (wind blowing into the landing), the boat can be halted parallel to the dock and a few feet from it. Then it will drift down to complete the landing. Bumpers are a necessity to protect a boat tied on the windward side and therefore subject to pounding. Approaching the leeward side of a dock, one must take wind resistance into account. Allow the bow to touch first and secure a bow spring line. Next turn the wheel away from the dock and put the outboard engine in forward gear to carry the stern up to the dock. Docking is not easy at first. Practice helps.

COMING TO ANCHORAGE

A mooring is best approached from the downwind and down-current side. When the wind and current are opposed, the preferred approach is into the stronger of the two. Although a mooring is less exacting to approach than a dock, the helmsman should attempt to bring his boat to a near stop at the moment the buoy is reached, so it can be picked up easily. Aboard boats with a low freeboard, a crew member merely reaches over the side and hauls the buoy, pennant, and mooring eye on deck. In larger craft a boat hook is used to capture the buoy. If the helmsman's view of the buoy is obstructed, he should take directions from the crew on the foredeck who uses hand signals to tell him when to turn to port or starboard. As soon as the mooring eye has been placed over the bow cleat, a quick shot of reverse will kill any remaining headway.

The operation is reversed when leaving the mooring. After eye, pennant, and buoy have been dropped over the side, the boat is backed downwind until the helmsman sees the buoy. Then he can steer a forward course to avoid it. At all cost, one should avoid running over a mooring. The result can be hours spent unfouling the line from the propeller. When leaving an anchor mooring and retrieving the anchor, the boat is aimed in the direction of the rode (anchor rope) leading into the water and moved ahead at slow speed. Someone on the foredeck hauls in the rode as it slacks and gives direction signals to the helmsman. When the boat is over the anchor, the bow man "breaks" it free from the bottom with a heave.

This boat demonstrates a good approach to a mooring. It is headed into the wind at slow speed but fast enough to control the steering. A boat hook is in use, ready to grab the mooring

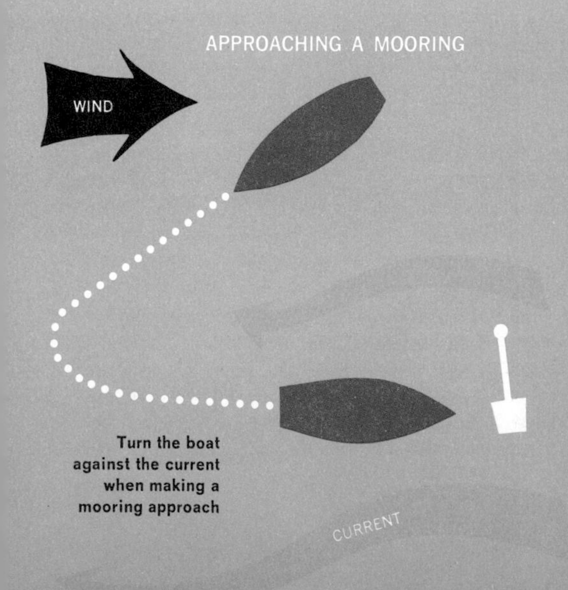

Turn the boat against the current when making a mooring approach

LEAVING & ENTERING SLIPS

Space is likely to be at a premium at the modern marina and taking a boat in or out of a slip may require skillful maneuvering in confined areas. Furthermore, wind and current will play upon the hull in the tight confines of the slip. Before starting up the engine, it is best to study wind and current, recognizing in what directions they will try to force the boat, and what steering compensations must be made. When wind and current are not factors, the task is easy—merely back straight out. Be sure to back all the way out, so the boat will clear the slip when making the turn to leave the mooring area. When returning, line the boat

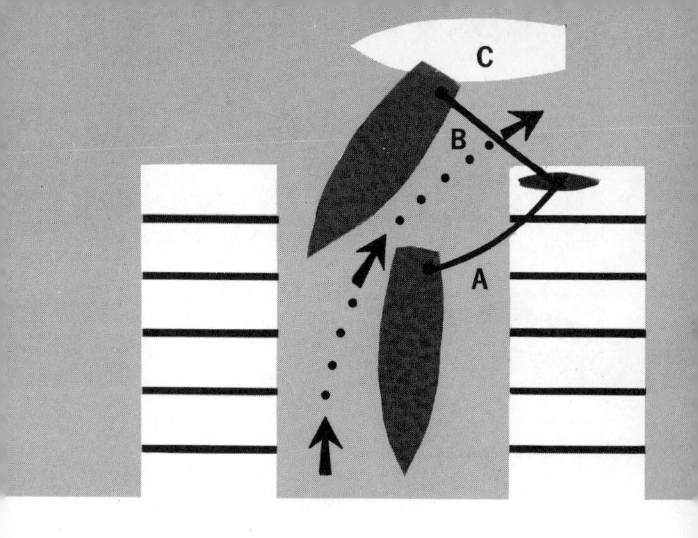

up parallel with the slip before entering it. Do not try to crab it in at an angle. This is the hard way.

In close quarters, use of one stern line will help to clear the boat from the slip safely and easily. Secure a line about two thirds the length of the boat to an outer piling at the corner or mouth of the slip (A in drawing above). The boat is backed down until the stern line goes taut (B), then the rudder is turned to clear the bow from the slip. At the same time, the stern line helps to pivot the hull away from the slip. When all is cleared (C), the stern line is freed. A controlled departure prevents banging the pilings.

LEAVING & ENTERING SLIPS

When wind and current are factors in entering a slip, the bow line can be used to pivot the boat about a piling. Approach the slip at right angles to it and secure a bow line to the first piling at the mouth. This line should be about two feet less than the width of the slip. The boat then continues forward until the line is taut. (Make sure too much forward momentum doesn't snap the line.) Next turn the wheel into the slip and go forward until the line has pivoted the boat in line with the slip. Cast off, straighten the wheel, ease into the slip, and tie up. This method is effective except when wind and/or current move against the stern of the boat. In this case, the same approach is made to the first piling at the mouth of the slip. Then both bow and stern lines are secured about the piling and pulled taut. The wheel is turned into the slip, the boat pivots, and the stern cannot be swung by wind or current across the slip into the opposite piling. The boat will proceed into the slip as the bow line is eased.

Left: The helmsman has carefully lined up his craft to enter a covered slip. Note the stern lines. They are secured to the slip rather than carried aboard. Below: A boat is tenderly backed into a stone pier. Lines are out and ready, bumpers in place to prevent scarring the topsides. And there is plenty of help for fending off

When beaching, pick a level, rock-free shore and tip the motor up

BEACHING

A nice advantage of an outboard-powered boat is that it can be beached on some sandy shore without damage to the propeller once the motor has been tipped free of the water. However, precautions should be taken in choosing the picnic site. Tide, for example. If there is a tidal rise and fall, recognize its action in the ensuing hours so that the boat will not be left high and dry when the shore visit is over. Also make sure the approach to the beach is free of rocks, which can cause havoc with the craft's bottom. The natural inclination is to ram the bow onto the beach, but don't do it. The safe way is to bring the craft into shallow water, step over the side, tip the motor up (after shutting it off), and ease the boat to the beach. To protect the stern from waves, beach the hull transom first.

Tow a dinghy with enough line out so it rides just aft the wake

TOWING

When towing another boat, the tow line and its correct length are the prime considerations. The tow line should be as substantial as a quarter- or half-inch anchor line and free from chafing. It is secured to a hefty cleat bolted through the deck, or to two cleats using a bridle. The craft being towed should have the line secured low at the bow. When towing begins, line is let out until operating speed is reached. Light dinghies tow best on the forward breast of the second following wave. Heavier boats ride best with their center just forward of the crest of the first or second stern wave, never on the afterbreast of a wave. A too-close tow may sleigh ride down the first wave into the towboat's transom. If a light dinghy yaws or "walks" over the wake, add weight in its stern to bring the bow up.

WHO HAS THE RIGHT OF WAY?

Rules of the road—the right-of-way rules—are the traffic regulations of the waterways. Since there are no red-light signals or traffic patrols afloat, every helmsman is expected to respect the rights of others and to obey these simple rules. In general, all boats without motors—those that rely on oars or sails—have the right of way over the more maneuverable power craft. So the first rule is to give rowboats and sailboats a wide berth. The wake of a passing powerboat can bring a racing sailboat to a virtual halt.

One of the common occurrences on the waterways is two craft closing head on. Sometimes an inexperienced sailor will panic and suddenly change his

A correct, port-to-port passing situation on the Inland Waterway

course, thoroughly confusing his opposite. The correct procedure is the same as on the highway: simply steer to the right and the other craft will do likewise. Rules of the road say that boats should steer to starboard and pass each other portside to portside. It is also common courtesy to slow down in a close passing situation. Low speed eliminates the necessity for each skipper to fight the other's wake. As an added safety precaution for boats passing port to port, the sound signal (one short blast of whistle or horn) is usually given as the two vessels approach. On open water, with several boat lengths between passing craft, signals and slow speeds are unnecessary.

WHO HAS THE RIGHT OF WAY?

The next right-of-way situation concerns two vessels closing on a collision course, at, or close to, right angles. The rule here is that the boat on the right-hand side has the right of way. The first is called the privileged vessel, the second the burdened one. The collision area is defined as the danger zone. It is measured at an angle of 112½ degrees from the bow to a point called in marine parlance "two points abaft the starboard beam." When the helmsman sees another vessel approaching within this angle from his bow, he must recognize that his is the burdened vessel, the other the privileged one. To repeat, when a boat approaches in the direction of the starboard bow, danger exists. The situation calls for the skipper to slow down, permitting the other to pass across his bow with plenty of room to spare, or to alter course, ending the possibility of collision. The privileged helmsman must be alert too, making sure the other skipper sees him.

When passing another vessel, the overtaken boat has the right of way and the overtaking one must keep clear until it is way beyond any danger of collision.

Below left: As these craft approach, the one to the right has the right of way. Below: The overtaking boat must keep clear.
Left: Passing boats are too close.
Both should bear off

Never speed through anchorages. By going slow, the boat's wake is at a minimum. Right: Be alert when leaving a dock. With other boats around, the situation can change rapidly. Avoid quick acceleration

WHO HAS THE RIGHT OF WAY?

Common sense plays an important part in the right-of-way rules and with boating customs. For example, a skipper should always throttle down when entering an anchorage or docking area. Waves from a high-speed wake can damage boats tied at docks. Many harbors have penalties for helmsmen violating their posted speed limits, usually five miles per hour or less. Care must be exercised around floats where people board their boats. Craft leaving docks are burdened to watch for boats in the waterway ahead before they too move out into harbor or channel traffic. Hot-rodding is out.

Too many small-boat skippers move out of the anchorage with an inflated sense of their own importance. Many want to challenge the Queen Mary in a right-of-way situation. While technically they may be correct, it is common sense for the smaller, more maneuverable boat to give way to the 80,000-ton liner, which may require a mile or more to come to a halt. Likewise, it is only common sense to give way to merchant vessels, warships, tugboats, barges, and other work boats that need a lot more room than pleasure boats. Stay alert at all times for situations threatening collision.

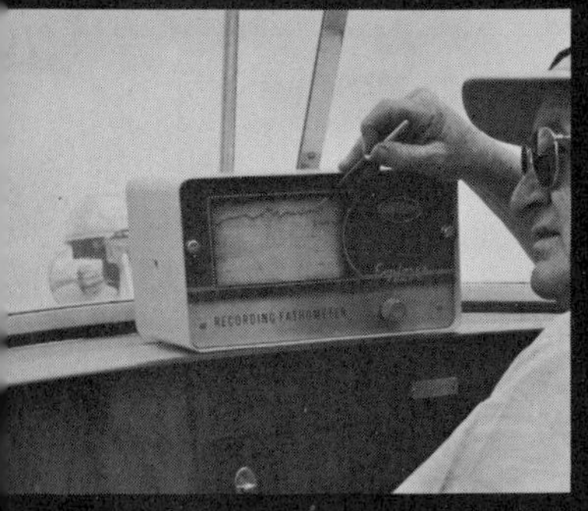

Fathometer records water's depth

Simple compass adjusts with coin

Plot the course for your voyage on the chart before leaving port

5

PILOTING

Charts and compasses are to the boatman what road maps and highway signs are to the motorist. By orienting the boat's location on a chart, it is possible to pick a second point and reach it by following the compass reading determined on the chart. A compact, inexpensive compass suitable for a small boat is graduated in units of five to 10 degrees. When a boat is steered to hold a compass course, this means that the dial hangs at a specific number, say 110 degrees, and the hull tracks a straight line over the bottom. But compasses are sensitive to nearby metal objects and electrical equipment that may cause a distortion of a few degrees. This is called deviation. If the distortion cannot be eliminated by isolating the compass, it must be measured and recorded on a deviation card. Such a card will tell how many degrees of correction to add or subtract when figuring the way to steer a specific course determined from the chart.

The navigational chart
is the road map of the waterways. The radio direction
finder (right) takes
bearings from radio beacons
shown on the charts (below)

PILOTING

All navigable waters of the United States, inland and coastal, have excellent charts prepared by the Corps of Engineers or the Coast & Geodetic Survey. Boatowners using waters not considered navigable will find useful topographical maps published by the U.S. Geological Survey. So there is no excuse for skippers going into unfamiliar waters without the proper charts. The wonderful, highly detailed navigation charts are available from Coast & Geodetic Survey offices (listed in metropolitan telephone books) or from map stores and marine supply houses serving as official agents. The abbreviated kind, free from oil companies, are not good enough for specific navigation and they say so.

The symbols on the charts, which convey a great deal of information in limited space, are simple but necessary to learn. The maze of numbers indicates depths at mean low water (average of low-water measurements). Buoys are pinpointed to show location and character—size, shape, color, number, lights, sounds. Shoals, rocks, wrecks, and other danger points are on the charts. So are prominent objects on land—church steeples, towers, tanks. Charts come in different sizes, the larger ones covering big areas and leaving out some detail. The smaller ones show everything. All are listed, by number, in a catalogue. Their cost is about a dollar apiece, making them one of the best bargains in boating.

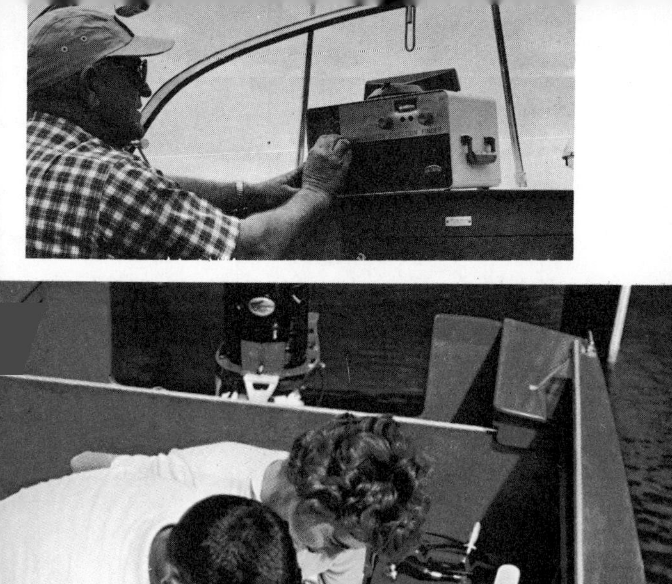

GOVERNMENT SERVICES

Government agencies print a number of publications invaluable to boatmen. Write to the sources listed below:

Coast and harbor charts. U.S. Coast & Geodetic Survey, Washington 25, D.C. Catalogue free.

Coast Pilots. Detailed data of coast lines and entry to harbors, 8 regional editions. Coast & Geodetic Survey, $2.50.

Tide Tables, Current Tables, Current Charts. Coast & Geodetic Survey, 50 cents and $1.

World-wide charts of off-shore and foreign waters. Hydrographic Office, U.S. Navy, Washington 25, D.C. Catalogue costs $3.

"Recreational Boating Guide." An 80-page Coast Guard booklet covering equipment, numbering, buoys, safety, etc. Superintendent of Documents, Government Printing Office, Washington 25, D.C., 40 cents.

Rules of the Road and Pilot Rules, Marine Inspection. U.S. Coast Guard, Washington 25, D.C.

Light Lists. Characteristics of all lighted aids, in 2 volumes. Superintendent of Documents, $3.25 and $3.

Charts of the Great Lakes and connecting waters, Lake Champlain, N.Y. State Canals, Lake of the Woods, Rainy Lake. U.S. Lake Survey, 630 Federal Building, Detroit 26. Mich. 25 cents to $1. Free catalogue.

Great Lakes Pilot. Harbor and piloting information supplemental to charts. U.S. Lake Survey.

Intracoastal Waterway booklets. Data on the waterway from Norfolk, Va., to the Rio Grande. In two sections. Superintendent of Documents, 65 cents each.

Charts of the Missouri River. U.S. Engineer Office, 1709 Jackson St., Omaha 2, Nebr., $1.50.

Charts of the Mississippi River. U.S. Engineer Office, 475 Merchandise Mart, Chicago 54, Ill., and Mississippi River Commission, P.O. Box 80, Vicksburg, Miss.

Illinois Waterway Book of Charts. U.S. Engineer Office, Chicago 54, Ill. $2.50.

Ohio River charts. U.S. Engineer Office, P.O. Box 1159, Cincinnati 1, O. In 3 sets. $2 each.

Tennessee River, Kentucky Lake charts. U.S. Engineer Office, P.O. Box 1070, Nashville, Tenn. Set $2.

Western States catalogue of boating facilities entitled "Reclamation's Recreational Opportunities," free from Dept. of Interior, Washington 25, D.C.

Canadian charts. Catalogues from Canadian Hydrographic Service, 249 Queen St., Ottawa, Can., 75 and 50 cents.

State Waterways. Write for free information from individual conservation departments, care of state capitals.

PLOTTING COURSES

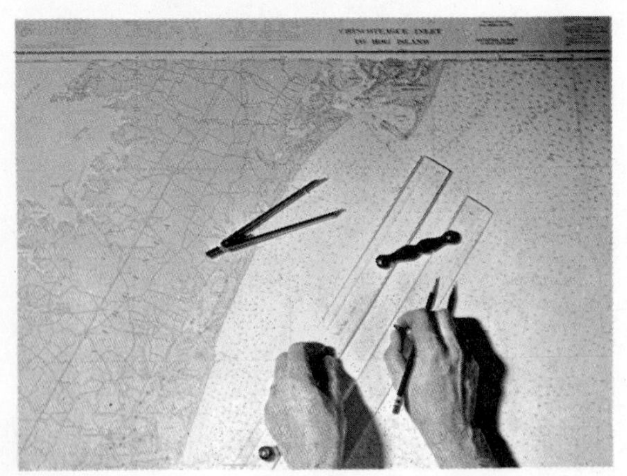

Chart a course with parallel rule, dividers

To plot a course on a chart one merely needs parallel rules, dividers, and a pencil. For practice, pick two points with open water between, so that they can be reached in a straight line. Using the parallel rules, draw in a line between the two points on the chart. Then "walk" (step) the rules from this line to the nearest compass rose. The latter, printed on the chart, has two circles of 360 degrees. Use the inner one, which has taken into account the magnetic variation (in degrees) caused by influences of the magnetic North Pole in the specific area of the map. The parallel rules should be so placed that an outer edge runs through

An offshore trip requires pinpoint navigation

the center of the compass rose and bisects the inner circle. The number of degrees it marks on the circle will indicate the course to be steered on the boat's compass. (But remember to apply the compass deviation correction, if any.) This figure should be written over the line on the chart, say 189 degrees. Next take the dividers and measure the length of the line. This length is applied to the scale of the chart, thus determining the distance in miles. The distance, say 3.0 miles, is written below the compass course under the line on the chart. To reach the second point, the boat is to be steered at 189 degrees for 3.0 miles.

PLOTTING COURSES

When it is not possible to go from point to point in a straight line, aids to navigation (buoys) shown on the chart come into play. Imagine a course of several straight lines between buoys, one after the other through channels, outside of islands and reefs, to the destination point. Each of these segments of the whole course is treated the same as the straight-line practice course. The compass direction and distance for each leg are plotted, using parallel rules and dividers, then written down on the chart. When each buoy is reached, the course changes. In plotting, be neat. Erase old courses so the chart may be used again.

It is possible to plot backwards, by taking line-of-sight bearings from the boat to objects shown on the chart. A simple cross bearing of two objects, when plotted on the chart, will determine the boat's location. Here is how a cross bearing can be figured. On

Navigator works in the cabin with charts and current tables, and on the bridge, searching the sea for a mark through powerful binoculars

shore two objects are visible—a church steeple and a water tower. The idea is to stand behind the compass and sight over it at the steeple, thinking in terms of an imaginary line between the two. Where the line cuts the compass dial, a bearing of, say, 270 degrees is determined. The compass deviation card says add five degrees, so, 275. Turning to the chart, the steeple is located. The parallel rules are laid over the compass rose, diametrically at 275 degrees on the inner magnetic circle. The rules are then walked to the steeple and the 275-degree line is drawn through the steeple and out over the water. The boat will be somewhere along this line. The same sight and bearing is taken for the second object, the tower, and drawn on the chart. Where the two lines intersect marks the location of the boat. In marine language, we have obtained a fix. For greater accuracy, a third bearing may be added.

MEASURING TIME, SPEED, DISTANCE

Piloting—the kind of navigation used by skippers on inland and coastal waters—is accomplished by observation and dead reckoning. Observation makes use of observed objects and their bearings to obtain fixes. When lines of position are unobtainable, as at night or in thick weather, the fix is determined by dead reckoning—meaning the navigator's best guess as to course, speed, sea conditions, current, and tide. It is not correct, but it is as correct as it can be until a fix by observation is obtained. Piloting, therefore, means a healthy combination, dictated by circumstances, of observation and dead reckoning. It solves the problems of navigation—that is, the problems of position, direction, speed, and distance. Distance as shown on charts is computed in nautical miles, which are longer than statute miles. A nautical mile measures 6,080 feet, or 1.15 statute miles.

Besides plotting courses and taking fixes, charts can be used to estimate the expected duration of a voyage, the distance already traveled at any time during a trip, and the actual speed of the boat over the bottom. Additional navigational tools needed are a stop watch and a fairly accurate speedometer. The way to predict the time a trip will take is to add up the miles as shown on the chart and divide by the average speed the boat can maintain. Thus, if the trip measures 60 miles and the boat cruises at 20 miles per hour, the trip can be made in three hours. Such a computation does not allow for tides or current, rough water, or poor

Check the speedometer by running a known course between buoys

visibility that will alter the speed. Compensations for these effects must be estimated. Most small-boat speedometers tend to be a little optimistic. That is, they show a greater speed than the boat is actually doing. The best way to check a speedometer is to run through a measured mile. These range stakes are found along many shorelines. They consist of two sets of twin targets which line up in pairs at a one-mile interval. The compass setting for the course is usually given on the chart. The best way is to run the course three times, starting the stop watch as the first targets line up with each other.

After completing the three runs, average the seconds for all, thus eliminating factors of changing tide and current. The average, say, is 130 seconds. Divide 130 into 3,600 (seconds in an hour) and the true speed comes out to 27.7 miles per hour. If the speedometer read 30 mph during the runs, the skipper now knows that the instrument exaggerates by 2.3 miles per hour when running in this general speed range.

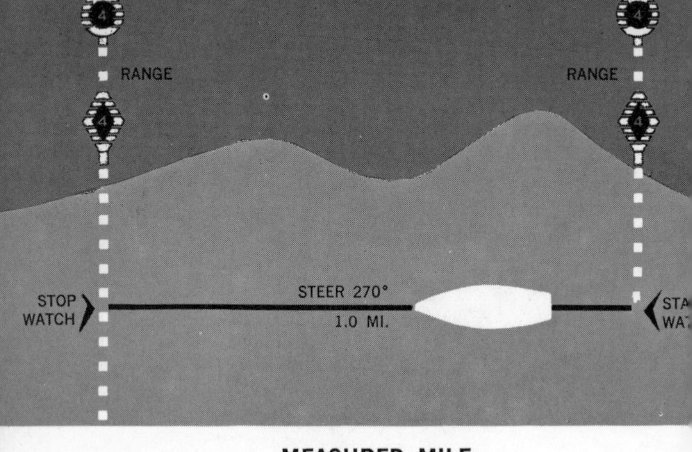

MEASURED MILE

MEASURING TIME, SPEED, DISTANCE

If a measured mile is not available, a speedometer can also be checked by running between two buoys after determining their distance apart from the chart. This will not be as accurate as the measured mile, because buoys are not always placed exactly as indicated on a chart.

Once the skipper has learned to plot a course, has an accurate compass, and knows the error in his speedometer, if any, he is in a position to tackle dead reckoning with confidence. Suppose visibility dims while he is two miles from a familiar buoy. Reducing speed to six miles per hour for safety's sake, he knows that to cover the two miles will take him about 20 minutes, or one third of an hour. Once he has found the buoy, he can plot his new compass bearing and move on to the next mark. Tachometers, which measure the revolutions of the engine shaft in per-minute

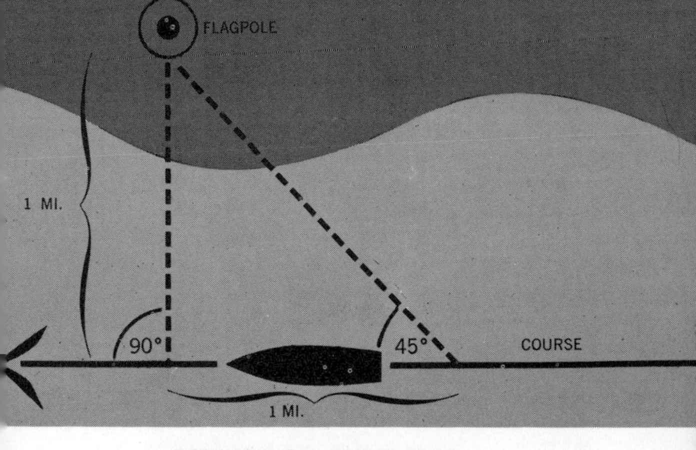

BOW-AND-BEAM BEARING

gradations can be used in place of speedometers. By running the boat through a measured mile at various rpm settings, a skipper can find the equivalent speeds in miles-per-hour terms and write them down on a conversion card. (1,200 rpms will equal nine miles per hour, as an example.)

Once speed is known, another means of taking a bearing becomes available. This is a good one: It is called a bow-and-beam bearing. When a permanent object, such as a flagpole on shore, bears 45 degrees from the bow, the time is noted. When the same object bears 90 degrees (at the beam), time is taken again. The distance run in the interval will be equal to the distance between the boat and the flagpole when the latter bears 90 degrees. If the interval is four minutes and the boat has been traveling 15 miles per 60 minutes, then the flagpole is one mile away.

AIDS TO NAVIGATION

This lighted bell buoy is painted red and therefore has an even number. Its opposite would be black and odd-numbered. Coast Guard sets and maintains the buoys

It would be difficult to drive cross-country without road signs to point the way. It would be even more difficult on the waterways if it were not for the buoyage system which aids navigation by marking channels, obstructions, dangers, and the best way home. The system calls for coloring, numbering, and shaping of various buoys in reference to the channels they define when such channels are entered from seaward. For example, when entering a harbor, all of the buoys on the port are odd-numbered and black, with flat tops

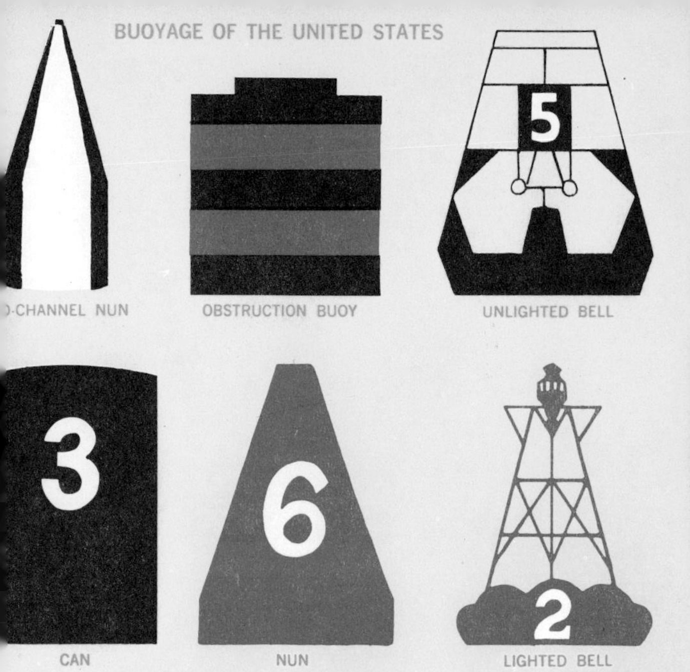

)-CHANNEL NUN OBSTRUCTION BUOY UNLIGHTED BELL
CAN NUN LIGHTED BELL

(cans), while those to starboard are even-numbered and red, with conical shapes (nuns). The opposite is true when leaving a harbor. The phrase "Red, Right, Returning," reminds the sailor to keep the red buoys on his right when returning to the harbor from seaward. On inland waters where "seaward" may confuse, running upstream is treated in the same manner as entering a harbor—meaning, pass the red nuns to starboard. Buoys with red and black stripes indicate a junction or obstruction. Pass them on either side.

Returning to port, keep the red nuns on the right, the black cans on the left. On the charts, the position of the lighthouse is fixed, its height, color of light, and distance of visibility described

AIDS TO NAVIGATION

The extensive Federal buoyage system is maintained by the U. S. Coast Guard and all the aids are shown on charts or in the Light Lists. Buoys can be simple red nuns and black cans or take more elaborate forms, such as bell buoys, gas buoys, spar buoys, lighted buoys, or combinations thereof. Buoys may be equipped with sound-producing devices, useful in fog. These include the trumpet or "groaner," bell, gong, and whistle. The more important buoys will have white, red, or green lights.

These aids are most effective in helping a helmsman to find his way—when used in conjunction with a chart. Buoys often mark danger points, but they should not be regarded as immovable objects. They can on occasion vary in position, especially in tidal waters, so it is not a good idea to pass them too close when they mark shallow water, rocks, or a reef.

There are many navigational aids besides buoys.

Lighthouses, unlike buoys, are in definitely fixed and known locations on land. Charts give information about the light, its characteristics, visibility, height above high water, and sound-making device. Lightships serve the same purpose as lighthouses and are different only in that they are floating lights at sea. Regular station ships have a red hull with the station name painted in white on the topsides.

Beacons are placed on shore or on sunken or awash obstructions where a floating buoy cannot be stationed. They may be of any shape: baskets, flags, triangles, cages, or arrows atop wood pilings, pipes, or rocks. Local marks of the same characteristics (including oil cans, wood floats, and fish stakes) are put out by local residents, supposedly with the approval of the Coast Guard or the harbor master, to mark channels not on the Government charts. They are not always accurate, so make local inquiry before believing them.

TIDE & CURRENT

Tide is the alternate rise and fall of ocean water governed by the gravitational pull of the moon and sun. Such waters are frequently spoken of as tidewaters to distinguish them from the inland seas or fresh-water lakes, which are not subject to this periodic variation of the water's surface. Current is the horizontal flow of the water. It is related to the vertical action of the tides, but also exists on non-tidal inland waters. The water through which a boat travels is not fixed (except on some inland lakes), but moves as a mass in accord with tidal and current laws. When a boat goes with the current velocity, its speed increases by the strength of the current. For example, a boat moving 12 knots in a two-knot current is moving over the bottom at a rate of 14 knots. (One knot equals one nautical mile per hour and current velocities are always measured in knots.) Conversely, a boat heading into a current will have its speed reduced by the strength of the current. The idea, therefore, is always to know which way the current is moving and when. If possible, plan the voyage to use this added push.

Tide and current actions can be determined by observation or from publications. To check which way the water is going, one should observe the flow past a fixed object, such as a dock piling or a mooring can. Government buoys are ideal. If the nun or can is leaning way over and the water is really gurgling by, the current is near its peak velocity. If the buoy is upright and there is no disturbance in the water around it, slack water is at hand and the tide is changing. It takes the experience of looking at many a leaning buoy to

Alongside a Maine dock at low water, showing tremendous rise and fall of the tide

estimate current velocities with any accuracy. However, the Government tide tables mark tide changes down to the minute and current velocities to a tenth of one knot. The tide tables tell the time on each day of the year when the tide will reach high and low water at a host of different locations. During a period of approximately 24 hours, 50 minutes, there will be two high tides and two low tides. On the charts, soundings are published in terms of mean low water, meaning the average depth of all low tides. The tide tables, in addition to giving the time of day of the highs and lows, also show the variations from mean low water.

TIDE & CURRENT

A high tide of 3.9 feet means the water will be 3.9 feet above mean low, while a low tide of –0.8 shows that the water level will go eight-tenths of a foot below the mean low-water mark.

Current tables perform the same functions, giving the four times during each day when the current is either slack or at maximum flow (flood), and also the velocity in knots at flood. Although current is likely to be slack (not running) at nearly the same time as when the tide has attained a high or a low, the relationship between the two and their timing varies slightly from place to place, so separate books of tables are needed. Current is more difficult to measure than tidal height and may be affected more by temporary conditions, such as wind or flooding. So the current tables are not necessarily gospel. There is also a marine classic called Eldredge's Tide and Pilot Book that has valuable information, in addition to tables.

These two boats are heading upstream, bucking a strong flow of current. If their speedometer readings are 10 miles per hour and the current running against them has a strength of five, then each boat's true speed over the bottom is reduced to five miles per hour

All courses and fixes, plus every feature of the chart, are shown, or drawn, in relation to the bottom, a static quantity. But water moves, so courses must be corrected by the amount of such movement and its direction. Suppose a boat is powering across a bay from west to east, but a two-knot current, moving from south to north, is pushing the craft at its beam. The helmsman must make a course compensation to balance this "set" of the current. If the voyage were to take two hours, the boat would end up four miles north of its intended destination. So the boat is steered on a course that would take it four miles south of its goal, had there been no current. In effect, the boat "crabs" along, much like an airplane in a cross wind, but it ends up at or near its destination. It must be acknowledged, however, that a perfect current-corrected course is hard to achieve and should be supplemented with observations and knowledge of local tides.

WEATHER

The red flag flying at left is the small-craft warning, forecasting winds and seas, or seas alone, dangerous to small-boat operation. Dark clouds like those below herald the coming of squalls, sudden wind shifts, and a storm. A red sunset (below right) gives promise of good weather on the morrow. All boatowners should learn to read and know the many weather signals

Boatmen live by the weather. Good weather means good boating and foul weather means trouble. Thanks to improved weather forecasting and quick communication of reports, small-boat owners can know what to expect from the weather on an hour-to-hour basis. Information is available in many forms: by telephone at no charge from any Weather Bureau or Coast Guard Station, from the reports in the daily press and over local radio stations, from flag signals at Coast Guard stations and boat clubs, and by means of the marine radiotelephone networks which provide the latest reports all day, every day. Then there is the barometer, indicating changes in atmospheric pressures, plus the skipper's own observation of the skies.

WEATHER

In the Northern Hemisphere, weather moves from west to east. The weather maps in the newspapers show the high- and low-pressure areas across the country and these can be expected to move east at a speed of about 600 miles each day. Generally, the weather in a high-pressure area is clear and dry, with gentle winds. Low-pressure areas are likely to be stormy, with humidity, rain, and stronger winds. The day during which a low-pressure area is due to arrive will not be an ideal one for boating. This will also be true on days when cold fronts (the convergence of hot and cold air masses) are scheduled to pass through. The locale, if not the exact time of the passing, can be determined from the maps. Cold fronts bring thunderstorms, often preceded by strong southwest winds. In weak frontal thunderstorms, wind, rain, and lightning are not severe or long lasting, but the more severe line squalls contain danger in the form of gale winds. And strong winds mean big waves. So know, from the forecasts, on what day the thunderstorm will arrive and, from the cloud formations, at what hour.

Clouds are good local weather signs. Light scud clouds alone indicate wind. Light scud clouds driving low under heavier cloud masses above indicate wind and rain. Small, black clouds foretell rain. Light, delicate clouds in fluffy masses mean fine weather. High clouds which move against the direction of the lower clouds indicate the future wind direction. A red sunset foretells tomorrow's fair weather. A sun halo heralds bad weather. A moon halo tells of changing weather, usually bad before good. When, after a fine-weather day, the sun sets behind cloud banks, rain may be expected within 12 hours.

A hard rain flattens the water and any breeze usually disappears

Cumulus clouds becoming lower and darker give storm warning

☐ According to the best available statistics, about 1,000 people drown each year as a result of boating accidents. That is why safety at sea, which can be a boring subject, is such an important one. On a cheerier note, almost every kind of boating situation that invites accident can be prevented by constant practice of safety at sea. This practice begins with recognition and knowledge of boating laws and regulations.

There are not too many of these, thank heavens, because boating is a sport of free spirits. However, the continued growth of boating (it was spectacular in the 1950's) will cause more crowding, and crowding brings regulation. Most of the present laws are the distillation of many years of U.S. Coast Guard experience in

THE RESPONSIBLE SKIPPER

small-boat problems. It is assumed that the amateur boatman must be willing to abide by these laws for the sake of himself, his passengers, and all others using the waterways. The alternative would be chaos, not safety, at sea.

Boating laws come from many sources on Federal, state, and local levels. The state laws usually cover registration, licensing, and safety equipment. They often parallel the Federal regulations that apply on all navigable waters. (The Coast Guard defines navigable waters as those which provide "a road" for transportation between two or more states or to the sea.) This is especially true of running lights, fire extinguishers, life preservers, signaling devices, and other safety equipment. County, township, or municipal laws usually pertain to local situations, such as harbor speed limits. State boating acts are administered either by conservation departments or wildlife commissions. It is a good idea to write these agencies (ask a local dealer for a specific address), requesting a booklet or pamphlet on your state's boating laws.

Boating law begins with registration and numbering of powerboats. Fees from registration support an enforcement program and in some cases provide for new facilities, such as launching ramps or marinas. All of the states excepting Alaska, Hawaii, Tennessee, Washington, and Wyoming, require registration and numbering of powerboats. In the exempted states, only those boats which will be used on navigable waters need apply. Application is made to the Coast Guard through blanks obtainable at local post offices. A registration number is then issued to the boatowner from the agency in Washington.

Note: In five additional states (Iowa, Maine, New Hampshire, New Jersey, and Pennsylvania) a dual form of registration is in effect. Boats berthed on the navigable waters of those states register with the Coast Guard. Those on non-navigable waters, such as inland lakes and rivers, apply to the state agencies.

Whether obtained from state sources or the Coast Guard, each boat's assigned number must be placed, in figures at least three inches high, on both sides of the bow of the craft in a legible color. A boat without a number and the accompanying certificate can cost its owner a $50 fine. In most cases registration must be renewed every three years, and when a boat is sold the issuing agency must be notified.

The next area of importance in boating law is the required safety equipment—lights, life preservers, fire extinguishers, etc. This varies from one state to another, but most adhere to the basic Coast Guard stipulations. However, on all navigable waters the Coast Guard rules controlling motorboat equipment do apply. In no case are Federal laws superseded by state equipment requirements. State regulations exist for boats on non-navigable waters outside of Coast Guard jurisdiction. Briefly, the Federal law requires: lighting for all motorboats; all motorboats, except outboards of open construction and under 26 feet in length, to carry fire extinguishers; all motorboats to carry at least one life preserver or ring buoy for each person on board (boats under 40 feet can use buoyant cushions or

Boat numbers must be at least three inches high and spaced well

vests); every motorboat of 16 feet or more to have an efficient whistle or other sound device; motorboats other than outboards to be equipped with carburetor flame arrestors; inboard motorboats to have ventilators capable of removing gases from the bilges in the engine and fuel-tank compartments, unless bilges are open.

So, in the areas of numbering and equipment requirements, Federal and state laws complement one another, giving as much protection as possible to boatowners. This is also true with regard to rules of operation, enforcement, and owner's liability. To show the extent of state boating regulations, there follows a digest of the laws in four of the larger boating states:

CALIFORNIA: All motorboats (and sailboats over 8 feet) register with Department of Motor Vehicles. Fee $5. Renewal every three years: $3. One to three fire extinguishers required, depending upon length of boat. Also whistle and bell, plus a life preserver for each person on board. Reckless operation prohibited. No person shall operate any motorboat while intoxicated. Accidents must be reported. Signals must be exchanged among passing boats. Owner's liability in the event of accident limited to $20,000. Violations subject to up to $50 fine and/or up to five days in jail.

FLORIDA: Motorboats over 10 hp register with Office of County Tax Collector. Fees, based upon boat length, $1.50–$10. All Federal equipment requirements apply. Reckless operation prohibited. No person shall operate any motorboat while intoxicated. All boats sold in state shall carry manufacturer's plate stating maximum horsepower and maximum load for safe operation. Overloading prohibited. Accidents must be reported. Coast Guard rules of the road apply. Liability for negligent operation confined to helmsman, not owner unless he is aboard. Conservation Department is the enforcing agency. Violations are subject to up to $75 fine.

MICHIGAN: All motorboats register with Secretary of State, or county sheriff's departments. Fee: $2 for three years. Equipment requirement confined to one bow light, distinguishable at 500 feet. However, Coast Guard equipment rules apply on Great Lakes and other navigable waters. Careless or reckless operation prohibited. Any person causing death of another by such operation shall be guilty of negligent homicide. Maximum penalty: two-year imprisonment, $2,000 fine. No person shall operate at a rate of speed greater than will permit him to bring the boat to a stop within the assured, clear, visible distance ahead. Accidents must be reported. Boatowner responsible for damages resulting from wake or swell created by negligent operation. Enforcement by county sheriff.

NEW YORK: All motorboats register with Division of Motor Boats. Fees: $3 under 16 feet; $6, 16-26 feet; $10, 26 feet and over, every three years. Equipment requirements similar to Coast Guard's. Five mph speed limits within 100 feet of shore. Accidents must be reported. Age of operators limited to 10 years and over. Ages 10-14 must take training course and hold safety certificate. Passing vessels shall exchange signals. Owner liable for damages due to negligent operation. Unlawful to deposit polluted matter into navigable waters. All peace officers, state or local, may enforce the Navigation Law. Violations are punishable by fine or imprisonment or both.

LIGHTS

Running lights are an important part of safety afloat as they announce the presence and direction of night traffic on the water. All boats operating after sunset are required to carry proper lights.

Coast Guard light regulations for motorboats use the "point" system. A light that can be seen in all directions (360 degrees) is a 32-point light. One that can be seen a little more than halfway around the light circle is a 20-point light.

On boats under 26 feet in length, the requirement is the single red-and-green combination bow light, shining 10 points on each of the color sides (red on port, green on starboard), plus a 32-point white stern light shining all around. An optional arrangement would be the 20-point combination light at the bow, an all-white 20-point light of three-mile visibility on top of the cabin or bridge, plus a 12-point white stern light.

In boats ranging from 26 through 65 feet, the regulations require: (1) a 20-point white light at the bow, (2) separate sidelights, red on port, green on starboard, showing 10 points from dead ahead, and (3) an all-around white light set higher than the others on the aft section of the cabin top. The white lights must have a visibility of at least two miles, the colored sidelights one mile. This is Coast Guard Option 1.

Option 2 calls for a 20-point white light of three-mile visibility set high atop the cabin or flying bridge; the separate 10-point sidelights as in Option 1, and a 12-point white light of two-mile visibility on a staff at the stern.

This boatowner prefers two white lights for maximum visibility

It is essential to keep a sharp watch for lights of other boats passing in the night. If a helmsman sees a red running light, he should change direction at once because he is heading into another boat's danger zone. Why? Remember that the red light is placed on a boat's portside and is so shadowed that it will be visible to another craft only when the portside is exposed. Going back to the rules of the road, the converging situation had two boats approaching, portside to starboard side, and the one on the right hand had the right of way. This vessel, therefore, would be showing its red portside light to the other. A red light appearing in a helmsman's danger zone is always a signal requiring a prompt response.

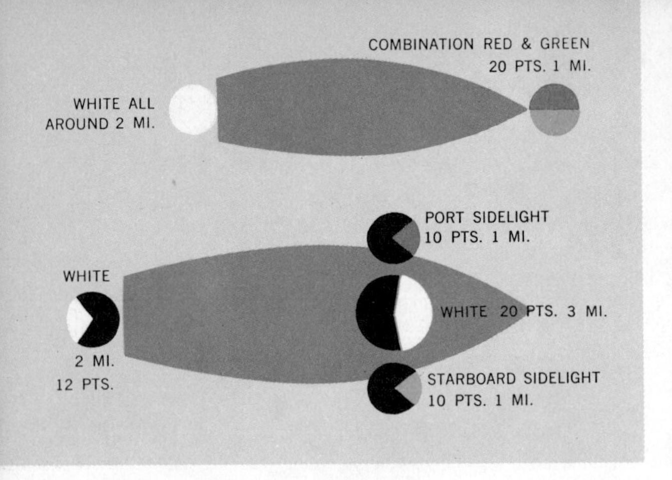

LIGHTS

The burdened craft, the one without the right of way, would expose her starboard green running light to the other, indicating no danger.

Unless a boat is in a recognized, special anchorage area, so designated by the Coast Guard or another such authority, it should carry a light when at anchor or at a mooring during the night. Anchor lights should be white, showing all around (32 points).

With considerable night boating experience, one can learn to identify the different light silhouettes and understand what they mean. Since almost all vessels will follow the Coast Guard regulations when placing their lights, and there are only four different combinations

An anchorage at night shows the
confusion of lights, as
those on shore blend with
the ones aboard oncoming boats

(under 26 feet, Options 1 and 2; 26 through 65 feet, Options 1 and 2), the comprehension of lighting systems is not too difficult.

However, the detection of these lights against a populated shoreline can be most difficult. A boat coming out from a well-lighted shore will be almost indistinguishable as its lights blend with those on land. In darkness, play safe and give a wide berth to moving lights. Speed should be greatly reduced at night.

Additional utility lights have great value on small boats. A spotlight helps to pick up moorings. A reliable flashlight can have a dozen uses, while cockpit lights make cruising enjoyable. Groping in the dark is no fun.

Hurricane! High water and violent winds have broken boats loose from their moorings and they are coming ashore to disaster

HAZARDS & DISTRESS

The troubles that can beset a boat are many—and serious. Explosion. Fire. Capsizing. Sinking. Collision. Running aground.

The usual reason for an explosion and its resulting fire is the ignition of the volatile gasoline fumes which collect so easily in the bilges of the hull. Precautions in fueling and the absolute necessity of ventilating the bilges have been discussed. Although outboard boats with their open bilges and, in most cases, removable gas tanks, are less prone to the threat of an explosion, there still is no reason to take chances when fueling. Boats under 26 feet should carry one portable extinguisher of the modern kind, using foam, carbon dioxide, or a dry chemical. "Dry" extinguishers smother flames in a cloud of inert powder.

Boats 26 to 40 feet should have two units, those from 40 to 65 feet should have three.

The cooking area (the galley) should be well ventilated and the stove bolted down, rather than portable. Who wants a portable fire?

Small boats capsize or swamp (fill with water) either because they are overloaded, or exposed to rough weather when they should be at home in port. The classic case of overloading happened a few seasons ago on a northern Michigan lake. There was one survivor among 13 people aboard a boat that capsized as the operator attempted to start the outboard motor. Those 13 people, adults and children, were passengers in a boat just 12 feet long. A 12-footer is normally overburdened with four occupants.

As for bad weather, a great deal of taxpayer money is spent each year by the Coast Guard and the Weather Bureau to circulate weather reports. Radio can keep most boatmen alerted to storms. The lack of a receiver is no particular excuse on waters near Coast Guard stations, boat clubs, or shipyards which fly the weather warning flags. When the triangular red flag is flying from a staff, boatmen should react as quickly as bulls. The flag's title, Small Craft Warning, is a literal one.

If a boat should capsize or swamp, life preservers, ring buoys, and buoyant cushions justify their existence. Most modern small boats have enough flotation material built into their hulls to enable them to stay afloat even when upside down or full of water. Therefore, the occupants of a capsized craft should stick with the boat and wait for help, rather than try to swim for shore.

The old and new. The sunken derelict finally succumbed

A leaking boat eventually will sink and it is a liability until the leak can be permanently stopped. However, few if any boat hulls are proof against punctures from collision, running aground on rocks, or striking floating debris. It is mandatory to keep a sharp lookout all around for debris when on the water. If a hull is stove in when underway, anything handy—rags, blankets, cushions, even clothing—should be stuffed in the hole. Floor boards can be used to help seal up split planking. When the bilges suddenly fill with water, locate the trouble quickly and do something drastic about it. Under these circumstances, the skipper who is prepared with a powerful hand pump aboard will have reason to be grateful.

There is little excuse for collision, but it happens frequently, anyway. The trouble may be that the use of the proper signals has gone out of style.

bad leak. The new hull can't sink, thanks to flotation tanks

Right: Explosion and then fire cruelly take their toll. Far right: The mooring line chafed away, leaving this craft to the mercy of the beach. Below right: A husky cruiser safely quarters the big seas at low speed. Bottom right: A Coast Guard rescue with helicopter and crash boat at the scene. The stricken vessel hit submerged rocks at high speed

HAZARDS & DISTRESS

Certain sound signals are universally used in this country. One blast of the horn is given when passing another boat in an orthodox manner, portside to portside. The privileged vessel (see Who Has the Right of Way?) initiates the exchange. When boats are far apart and passing starboard to starboard is more practical, two blasts are exchanged. An overtaking boat gives one blast when passing the vessel ahead on its starboard side, two blasts when on the portside. These and other signals should be answered by repeating them. In any passing or overtaking situation, when one vessel does not consider the intended maneuver to be safe, it should give a series (not less than four) of quick blasts. In fog, vessels should sound their horns or bells at regular intervals.

The common excuse for running aground is ignorance of the area. But with all the excellent charts and/or abundant local advice available, such a plea is unacceptable. The only answer when aground is to wait for the next high tide; to try to back off, using full power; or to push off with the boat hook.

POLICING THE WATERS

Enforcement officers in boats are becoming more numerous and their roles more diversified as nautical traffic increases. Their purpose is to enforce the marine laws, but at heart they exist to make the boating scene safer and more equitable for everyone.

The Coast Guard is the Federal arm. This is an agency with many duties, of which recreational boating can be only a part. Its area of responsibility is all the thousands of miles of navigable waters, its manpower is thin for the task, its budget problems per-

State and local officials are active patrolling many waters and enforcing the boating law. As registration money becomes available, these teams will increase. Here an inspection of safety equipment is underway with emphasis on cushions

manent. In a recent year, two eastern Coast Guard districts answered 9,002 calls for assistance. The Third District, with headquarters in New York, spent 11,000 hours in search and rescue work, a great deal of it involving pleasure boats that had become lost or had run out of gas. The latter situations are truly exasperating.

In places where the Coast Guard either lacks jurisdiction or the manpower for patrol, state, county, and municipal officers try to fill the gap. With passage of the Federal Boating Act of 1958 and the increase

of state registration fees, more money has become available for the hiring and equipping of enforcement personnel on local levels. In New York, for example, half of the registration fees are available in the form of state aid to counties having water-patrol programs to enforce the law.

In addition to law enforcement, these peace officers can be of immense help in arranging a share of the available waters. On many inland lakes, different kinds of water sports have different needs and are in-

**The Coast Guard is the Federal arm of the waterways.
Far left: A rugged CG surf boat.
Below left: A lightship, a 95-foot cutter, and a helicopter—all part of the CG fleet.
Left: The Coast Guard Auxiliary conducts a courtesy exam**

compatible when cast together at close quarters. Fishermen, who seek solitude, and water skiers, who destroy it, are often at odds. The best solution is to designate specific areas for these activities, the adherents of each to stay away from the other's water. But such a solution requires persons in authority to make it stick. So the cop in the boat can be a helper.

Two civilian organizations merit attention, the U.S. Power Squadrons and the Coast Guard Auxiliary. Both are composed of devoted boatmen and their greatest service is the vast educational program that each conducts. The USPS and the CGA give classes, free and open to all, which teach the fundamentals of boating, with emphasis on safety. Notice of the courses usually appears in local newspaper boating columns. The Auxiliary, furthermore, will perform a courtesy examination, free upon request, of any pleasure boat. These inspections check a craft's safety equipment and general seaworthiness. CGA flotillas are located in hundreds of communities and a telephone call to any one of them will bring a volunteer inspector, an expert amateur boatman, to make an examination and to recommend any needed improvements. Boats that pass receive a windshield decal which usually exempts them from being boarded by the Coast Guard.

LIABILITY & INSURANCE

Marine insurance has hedged the risks and perils of sea voyages for centuries. It is still a wise investment for the boatowner today. Many hazards, such as pirates, have disappeared, but others—fire, lightning, windstorms—still threaten and some new ones have arisen from the complexity of modern life. Here are random claims paid by a Midwest insurance company: Loss of an outboard motor dropped overboard while mounting it. Vandals chopping a hole in a boat. Boat catching fire, while on a trailer, from a cigarette tossed by a passing motorist. Wind blowing down a tree, crushing a boat. Trailer overturning, damaging boat and motor. A friend borrowing a boat and running it aground on a rocky shore. A boat swamped by a passing tug; motor damaged by salt water. A boat in a garage damaged by boatman's wife parking the car.

Marine insurance will protect against collision with a fishing craft or liability from injuring a skin diver

These are only a few of the misfortunes that can befall a boat. Therefore, be protected with insurance. Policies are many and variable; check before you buy.

Generally, for the small boat there are three forms of insurance in force. These are: 1) Limited Named Perils Insurance, 2) Broad Named Perils Insurance, and 3) All-Risk or Comprehensive Insurance. All three cover physical loss or damage to outboard motors, boats, and trailers. In some instances a certain amount of coverage applies to damage done to the property of others. The first kind names the perils it will cover: fire and lightning, collision or overturning of a loaded trailer; windstorm on land only; theft of boat and motor. The loss suffered must be caused by one of these perils or there can be no recovery.

The second type adds collision with another vessel

or object while water borne, and the traditional perils of the sea (loss or damage due to grounding, sinking, windstorm, hurricane, lightning, striking obstructions, or other vessels). The All-Risk or Comprehensive policy insures against almost every occurrence, usually on a deductible basis, with the insured paying the first $25 to $100 of the claim. The deductible feature is in most policies for the purpose of avoiding petty claims. The rates for this kind of a policy run around $4 per $100 of the value of boat, motor, and equipment ($2 for trailers).

A motorboat is a dangerous instrument with a propeller that can kill, maim, and injure, so every responsible owner should carry personal liability insurance. In 22 states, boating laws say civil liability applies to boatowners. Personal liability coverage comes separately from most physical-loss policies. In some instances, comprehensive personal liability coverage or homeowners' policies will cover owners of small boats. However, because of the expansion of boating and the resulting rise in liability claims, insurance companies are tending these days to add specific endorsements to policies covering boats of ten horsepower or more, and to charge an extra fee of $10 to $40.

Racing, through the parent American Power Boat Association, has provided its own insurance for competition drivers, who face extraordinary risks.

Insurance is a protection in case something goes wrong. The practice of safe boating habits is the best prevention against something going wrong. The insurance companies recognize this, and have undertaken large information programs to help educate the boating populace in safety measures and precautions.

This race boat turned over, killing its driver

Water skiing requires an observer to watch behind

7

YOUR NEXT BOAT

☐ Rare is the man whose first boat is his last. There is no thrill quite like the first purchase but, more often than not, ownership is a matter of trial and error. Despite good intentions, the novice buyer is likely to find after a couple of seasons that what he has is not quite what he needs. By this time he is an old salt with a keener appreciation of a boat's limitations. Statistics show that the second buy is likely to be a boat with a little more room, a little more power, and a little more comfort.

When in the market for a first boat, or a trade-in, these considerations are important: 1) Principal use—fishing, water skiing, family outings, day cruising, live-aboard vacations, or a combination thereof.

National Motor Boat Show at New York in 1907

2) Water conditions–hull design and size requirements vary according to the type of water (river, protected lake, large lake, offshore). 3) Load demands –size of the family, fishing gear, water-ski equipment. 4) Mooring or trailering–will the boat live on the water or will it be hauled back and forth from a launching site? 5) Money–the size of the family boating budget. If the first-time buyer can determine these specifications for himself, he has a reasonable guide and is likely to make a satisfactory choice.

The best place to look the fleet over is at a boat show, and there are dozens of these held in principal cities. Under one roof, the party with an itch to buy can size up several models, compare features and prices. The larger boat shows can be bewildering exhibitions. It takes planning to check their inventory of displays. The sensible way is to mark in the show directory the exhibits that seem to fit the plan of purchase,

A modern show fills New York's Coliseum to capacity

then start a tour. Take along a knowledgeable friend who recognizes quality. There are good boats, there are bad boats, and in this sport, probably more than in any other, quality will be the cheapest feature one can buy in the long run. A boat show is a good place to look, but not necessarily a good place to buy. A craft's performance in the water cannot be evaluated in a bone-dry exhibition hall. So make mental notes, but hold off buying until a dealer back home can give a demonstration of performance afloat.

Prices may vary throughout the show. Some companies may offer boats at comparatively low prices, but without essential "extras." Fortunately, there is a trend among responsible manufacturers to set a price that includes such basic equipment as steering gear, windshield, and hardware. When comparing prices, it is essential to evaluate manufacturers' standards and extra equipment. Now for a look at some dreamboats.

DREAMBOATS

DORSETT: This runabout employs conventional engine with Berkeley jet-drive propulsion unit, eliminating the propeller. Dorsett Marine, Santa Clara, Cal.

BERTRAM: The very fast 31-foot sport cruiser has smooth-riding V-hull, twin engines of 275 hp each. Prices start at $16,000. Bertram Yacht Co., Miami, Fla.

ALUMA CRAFT: A 16-foot day boat with hard top. Hull construction is aluminum. About $1,000. Aluma Craft Boat Co., Minneapolis, Minn.

PONTOON: A wide variety of manufacturers turns out this type of pontoon craft with sun deck, outboard motor. Use is restricted to quiet waters

GLASSPAR: The Seafair Phaeton is a 17½-foot outboard cruiser priced at $1,845, less motor. Fiberglass hull has 7-foot beam. Glasspar Co., Santa Ana, Cal.

LAKEFIELD: A small boat for fishing, this craft has wood-planked hull suitable for outboards up to 25 hp. Lakefield Boats Ltd., Lakefield, Ont.

DREAMBOATS

TURBOCRAFT: Jet 35 has 18½-foot fiberglass hull, 200-hp engine with jet-drive unit replacing propeller. Buehler Corp., Indianapolis, Ind.

FLYING FINN: Seafin 19 hull is lapstrake, pine-planked, built in Finland. A rugged craft for outboards up to 80 hp. Flying Finn, 527 Lexington Ave., NYC.

SQUALL KING: A 17-foot fiberglass cruiser, easy to operate with twin 40-hp outboard motors as shown. Continental Boat Corp., North Miami, Fla.

WHIRLWIND: Roomy 16-foot runabout called Rocket is low priced at $659. Will take outboards up to 80 hp. Molded Products, Cockeysville, Md.

MATTHEWS: A luxury craft with twin 225-hp engines, this 52-foot flying-bridge cruiser with eight berths costs $76,500. Matthews Co., Port Clinton, O.

THUNDERBIRD: Scout sport fisherman of fiberglass has unique inverted V-bottom. Length is 19 feet, cost $2,695. Plastic Fabrications, Hialeah, Fla.

DREAMBOATS

LONE STAR: Outboard-powered Vacationer has 17-foot fiberglass hull, costs $1,695 less motor. Roomy cabin sleeps two. Lone S Boat Co., Grand Prairie, Tex.

CRESTLINER: The 14-foot open utility has aluminum hull designe for fishermen, weighs only 180 pounds. Rides on car top. Crestl Inc., Little Falls, Minn.

SWIFT: This 16-foot utility runabout is of plywood hull construction. Can take outboards up to 70 hp. Swift Boat Division, Mt. Dora, Fla.

CARTER CRAFT: Day cruiser measures 15½ feet in length. Hull is plywood. Maximum outboard horsepower is 75. Carter Craft Corp., Panama City, Fla.

MFG: The 15-foot fiberglass open fisherman weighs 475 pounds, takes outboards up to 40 hp. About $800. Molded Fiber Glass Boat Co., Union City, Pa.

BAY HEAD: Custom sport fisherman built to order is rugged offshore craft with lapstrake hull, twin engines. N. J. Yacht Sales, Pt. Pleasant Beach, N. J.

DREAMBOATS

PENN YAN: This 14-foot utility, powered by 15-hp outboard, can go 20 mph. Hull is canvas-covere cedar, 210 pounds, about $700. Penn Yan Boats, Penn Yan, N. Y.

HOUSEBOATS: These models, o steel and aluminum, are outboar powered, can cost from $2,500 to $8,000. Spaciousness, not speed, is attraction of these boats.

LARSON: Ready for the highway, Sea Lion cruiser (left), about $1,900, and 16-foot runabout, $1,200. Both are fiberglass. Larson Boats, Little Falls, Minn.

LYMAN: A plywood, lapstrake runabout, this 18-footer takes an outboard up to 80 hp; hull costs about $1,290. Lyman Boat Works, Sandusky, O.

HYDRODYNE: Fiberglass 17-foot hull is powered with Volvo 80-hp inboard-outboard unit. Has hydraulic-action seats, $2,870. Midwest Industries, Harlan, Ind.

DREAMBOATS

COLONIAL: Sport Fisherman has dual controls, flying bridge, twin engines, galley, sleeps six; about $32,270. Colonial Boat Div., Millville, N. J.

GRUMMAN: G-19 Sportser utili is all-around outboard-powered aluminum craft with 100 hp maximum. Price for hull: $1,950 Grumman Boats, Marathon, N.

CHRIS-CRAFT: Cavalier Custo 25-footer is inboard cruiser with 100-hp engine, $4,945. Cavalier Div., Chris-Craft Corp., Pompano Beach,

POWER CAT: This 15-footer has catamaran hull of fiberglass. About $1,200, with outboard horsepower of 90. Power Cat Boat Corp., Paramount, Cal.

CARVER: This group of outboard runabouts has molded plywood hulls, 15 to 20 feet in length. Prices run $900 to $2,000. Carver Boat Corp., Pulaski, Wis.

CHRIS-CRAFT: The 45-foot Constellation cruiser has complete cruising facilities, twin engines. Prices begin at $45,000. Chris-Craft, Pompano Beach, Fla.

DREAMBOATS

CENTURY: Coronado 21-foot runabout has mahogany-planked hull, seats for nine, speed to 55 m with 325-hp engine, $6,350. Century Boat Co., Manistee, Mich

PACEMAKER: A quality boat at about $24,000, this 40-footer can roam far offshore on fishing trips. C. P. Leek & Sons Egg Harbor, N. J.

SICA: This 25-foot Family Cruiser has galley, hull of mahogany lapstrake, single engine of 135 hp, sleeps four. Sica Skiffs, Toms River, N. J.

HATTERAS: Husky cruiser has 34-foot fiberglass hull, 12½-foot beam. Twin engines give up to 560 hp. Hatteras Yacht Co., High Point, N.C.

STEPHENS: A 47-foot custom cruiser with all-electric galley, air conditioning, twin diesels, walk-around deck, $86,000. Stephens Marine, Stockton, Cal.

OWENS: A 29-foot Express Cruiser featuring mahogany double planking, twin engines of 290 hp. Price is $12,495. Owens Yacht Co., Baltimore 22, Md.

An attractive show space, whether indoors (right) or out (below), helps a customer to inspect his dealer's nautical wares

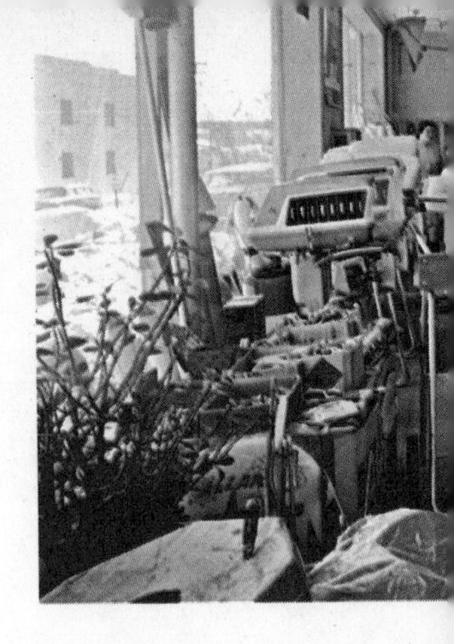

DEALERS & DOLLARS

Choosing a dealer is by far the most important decision a prospective buyer has to make. A boating outfit is seldom "bought" in the usual sense of the word. Rather, it is put together, component by component, and designed for the customer by the dealer. There are hundreds of makes of boats, a bewildering variety of "body styles" and sizes in different materials. Just about everybody claims the best designs, the best performance, the best buy. A reputable dealer, seriously interested in his customer's welfare, can separate claims from facts.

Costs? A new 14-foot outboard runabout, with room for four and some gear, will cost from $400 to $600. An outboard motor in the 18-22 horsepower bracket is $400-$450. A trailer sells for $150, accessories $50. So the package price for this modest rig comes to $1,000

Power sander helps when taking an old boat down to bare wood

plus. The scale goes up from there. Divide the price by the useful life of the outfit—say four years—to establish the cost per year. Add the yearly amount needed for fuel, insurance, and maintenance (a good dealer can give an estimate). These two figures combined give the total annual cost of owning and operating a boat. Most outfits are purchased with a payment of 10 to 20 per cent at the time of delivery. The balance is financed out of monthly income. Dealers or banks can arrange time-payment plans.

Boats and motors depreciate according to established schedules. Most inboards lose 25 per cent of their list price the first year, then 33, 40, 45, and 50 per cent in following years. So a five-year-old inboard is worth about half its initial cost. These generalities seldom apply to some very popular types, which do not change from one year to the next. Outboard boats have a heavier scale of depreciation: 30 per cent the first year, 50 per cent after two seasons, and up to 75 per cent when five years old. As for outboard motors, the leading brands depreciate 50 per cent in value the first year, but then the schedule slows, to 54, 58, 61, and 67 per cent in ensuing seasons. Lesser brands drop off more rapidly and will lose 83 per cent of initial list price by the end of five years.

There are bargains to be had in used boats, but buyer beware! It takes an expert to size up a used boat accurately because many faults are hidden to the eye. Here is what to look for. With wooden hulls, check the planking for cracks, splits, and broken ribs. The blade of a penknife can quickly probe for the soft pulp in wood planks. This indicates dry rot, which is bad news. Bubbles in paint warn of a cover-up job. A poorly painted surface probably means the hull will have to be taken down to bare wood, an expensive and time-consuming process. On fiberglass hulls, look for surface cracks. Once they start, they are hard to stop. Check the inside for signs of patches, indicating a hull puncture. Investigate the way in which wooden seats, elbows, transoms, and decks are joined to the hull, whether wood or glass. These can work loose and weaken the craft. Does it leak? Pour a bucket of water into the hull and see. On aluminum boats, search for loose rivets. They spell leaks. Motors, outboard or inboard, are more difficult to check, but unrealistic "deals" are to be avoided. In the final analysis, the used-boat buyer will have to count on his dealer's good faith and responsibility.

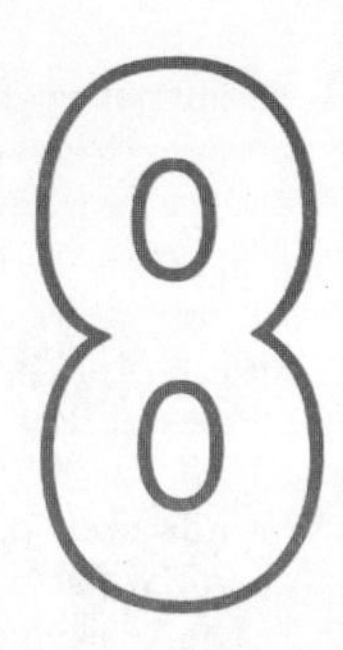

CARE & MAINTENANCE

Preventive maintenance is the lifeblood of boating. Consistently applied, it will help the boatowner get the most out of his sport. Otherwise, he will spend his time in the yard or engine shop waiting for the boat to become seaworthy again. Some owners baby their craft, but too many others spend less time on their boats than they do on their cars. The fellow who would not consider driving 1,001 miles without an oil change will leave his boat uncovered and untended for a week, never thinking to have the engine inspected or overhauled until the day it breaks down and he becomes a towing statistic for the Coast Guard. Boats are not indestructible. Maintenance is a good habit to cultivate

Hood flips open permitting access to outboard motor's vital parts such as carburetor and spark plugs. Plugs are easy to change and powerhead requires minimum lubrication during a season's operation

CARE & MAINTENANCE

Maintenance can mean many things. The way to begin is by setting the rig up properly and tuning the motor so that trouble will not strike later. With an outboard, this means proper placement of the motor, balance of the load, and correct selection of the propeller. The best rule of thumb regarding the placement of the motor on the transom is to set the cavitation plate in line with the bottom of the boat. This horizontal plate lies above the propeller on the lower unit of the motor. When correctly placed, the water will flow freely past the lower unit, minimizing drag. A motor set too high on the transom will cavitate—meaning that the propeller will break free of the water's surface, resulting in loss of power and an awful racket. A motor placed too low will cause the bow to bury. Every outboard has a selection of pinholes low down on the motor bracket which permit adjustment of the vertical tilt of the motor. The lower unit fits snugly against the bracket, which in turn secures the motor to the transom.

Far left: It takes two to mount the motor safely, from dock to transom. Center: This motor's vertical tilt is all wrong, wasting power. Left: Motor with correct tilt adjustment

The correct tilt adjustment is vital to performance. If the cavitation plate is absolutely in line with the bottom of the boat, and the lower unit is perpendicular, the correct pinhole has been chosen.

Balancing the weight in the boat is most important for outboards, less so for heavier inboards. A load too far forward will cause the bow to bury. One too far aft will make the boat difficult to manage and may even push the bow high out of the water, thereby limiting the helmsman's visibility.

On small outboards—10 horsepower and below—the standard, multi-purpose propeller is fine. With larger rigs, it is a good idea to try to match the right sized propeller with the weight of the boat and the job it is expected to do. The determining factor is propeller pitch, a measurement of the small distance the propeller will travel through the water when making one revolution. The lower the pitch, the greater the pulling power and the higher the resulting engine speed.

Higher-pitch props, traveling a greater distance through the water on each revolution, are used for lighter boats and higher speeds. A prop with too low a pitch, however, may permit the motor to accelerate beyond its capabilities. This is called "winding-up," and a motor with an intended ceiling of 4,500 rpms may damage itself when turning, say, twice that fast. Propellers are a complex subject for the beginner and a dealer's advice and chart can be most helpful in getting the right one.

When a boat has been completely rigged for the new season, it is a good idea to go over it, checking all the connections, fastenings, and clamps. Gear can work loose in rough water or at high speeds, and the inevitable result will be a breakdown—the surest way to take the pleasure out of boating.

Below: A check of cruising equipment, but where are the extra fuel tanks? Right: This twin-engine installation provides easy access, flush-deck cockpit

When planning a voyage, it is nice to know how much fuel to take along. The larger outboards can consume more than eight gallons of fuel each hour when operating at full speed. Outboard engines are of two-cycle design, simple in character, but thirsty for fuel. The four-cycle inboards are heavier, more complex and expensive, but thriftier with fuel. Outboard fuel is a mixture of oil and gasoline, and it is important to be sure they are thoroughly blended. The oil lubricates the moving parts in the powerhead as the fuel passes from the carburetor to the pistons. The propeller casing requires lubrication through a grease point on the lower unit.

The Federal Government and many states permit boatowners to file for rebates of taxes on gasoline used for boating. Save sales slips as evidence.

A

B

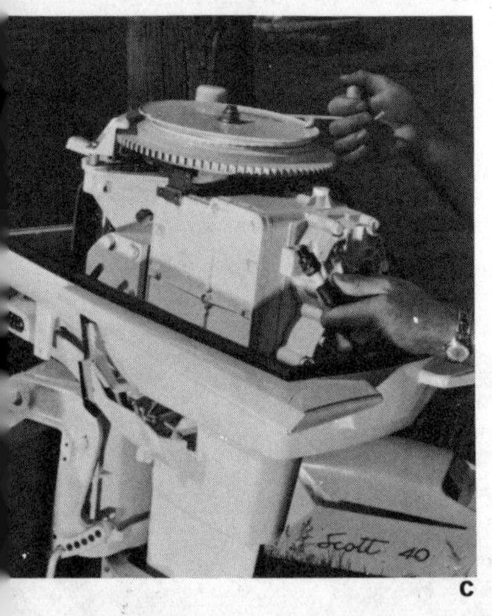

C

(A) Use a wire brush to clean corrosion from battery terminals. (B) There are special lubricants for lower gear casings. (C) Test the spark by grounding the plug. (D) Measure the important spark plug gap with feeler gauge

D

The fuel, electrical, and cooling systems in an outboard motor require periodic maintenance. Filters in the fuel lines should be cleaned after every 10 hours of running. It is a good idea to run the fuel tanks dry from time to time, then examine the bottoms for dirt and rust. If any is found, tanks can be flushed clean with a bit of kerosene. Water may also accumulate in fuel tanks. If so, flushing them with commercial alcohol will remove it.

The key to an outboard's electrical system is the spark plug. Because outboard plugs tend to foul, they should be checked after every 25 hours of operation, cleaned and re-gapped if necessary. If the gap at the base of the plug is too small, there will be a tendency for the plug to foul with oil from the fuel mixture. If the gaps are too great, starting will be hard and running erratic. Gaps can be tested with the feeler gauge usually supplied in new motor tool kits. At longer intervals, all ignition wires should be checked for worn insulation. If the motor has an electric starter, it will have a wet-cell battery which needs cleaning, filling, and perhaps charging.

Salt water is no friend of the outboard motor. Corrosion eventually will pit and scar it, despite the manufacturers' assurances to the contrary, unless the unit is cleaned often with fresh water. Outboard cooling systems have flushing nozzles to which a garden hose can be attached. After salt-water use, the preventive maintenance is to flush out the cooling system with fresh water from the hose. Another way, for those motors that lack a nozzle, is to run the outboard for a time in a tank of fresh water. The result is the same—the salt deposits are washed away.

Check ignition wires and connectors for wear and corrosion, propellers for bent blades and dents along the edges

A boat and motor are better off when in use than when idle, so out-of-season storage is an important part of motor maintenance. The first step is to empty the motor of both fuel and water. After the last trip of the season, when the outboard is still on the transom, it should be run at half-throttle with the fuel line disconnected until it burns the remaining fuel in the carburetor. One manufacturer recommends that an internal corrosion and rust preventative be injected into the carburetor air intake as the motor is running down, to protect piston and cylinder walls. Next, the motor should be taken off the transom in an upright position so that all the water will drain out. Turn the manual starter over a few times to make sure all water ejects from the cooling system. Winter ice inside an outboard can cause havoc.

Take the spark plugs out, inject about an ounce of rust and corrosion inhibitor in each hole, and put the plugs back again. Remove the steering cables, also the remote throttle-gearshift controls, and store them in a single box. The propeller should come off and its shaft cleaned with steel wool or sandpaper (not emery cloth). Then apply graphite or silicon grease to the surfaces and put the propeller back. If there is a battery, corrosion around the terminal posts must be cleaned out, distilled water added, and a charge put on if necessary. Batteries are best stored in dry places not subject to temperature extremes. The outboard, too, should be kept in a clean, dry place, covered, but with enough air circulation to prevent moisture accumulation. When the various preventatives are removed in the spring, the motor will be in good shape to start the new season.

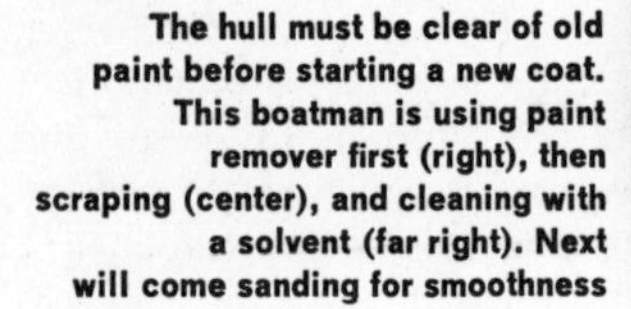

The hull must be clear of old paint before starting a new coat. This boatman is using paint remover first (right), then scraping (center), and cleaning with a solvent (far right). Next will come sanding for smoothness

PAINTING

Pride of ownership is a wonderful tradition of boating, pride which has its first reflection in a craft's appearance. This tradition is best expressed with the annual painting of all wooden boats before a new season begins. Almost all will need new paint, both for appearance and hull protection. Even fiberglass and aluminum boats, whose adherents boast "no maintenance," will require painting eventually if they are to retain their original smart look.

Painting a boat is not hard labor, but preparing it for paint can be. The options are simple—do-it-yourself, or pay someone else to do it. The secret of any good paint job is a good surface, a smooth one that will absorb the new coats evenly. Because of the tortures boats go through, special high-quality marine paints are required. Cheaper house paint won't do.

Prepare the hull by sanding it down, either by hand or with power, using filler to cover scratches and dents. About every three seasons the hull should be taken down to bare wood, and all old paint removed with sandpaper and chemicals. The acid from the paint remover must be neutralized with a base such as

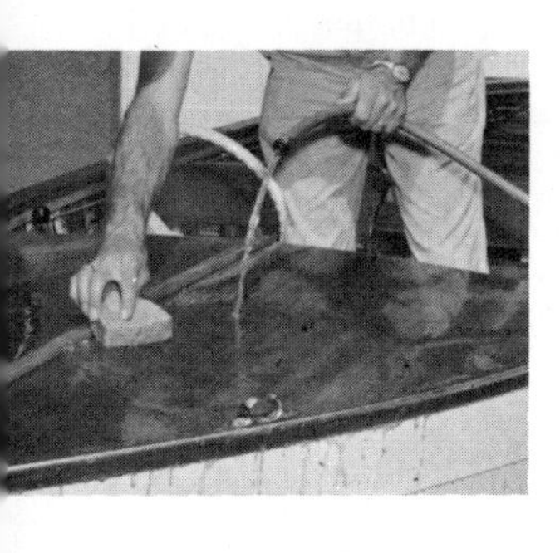

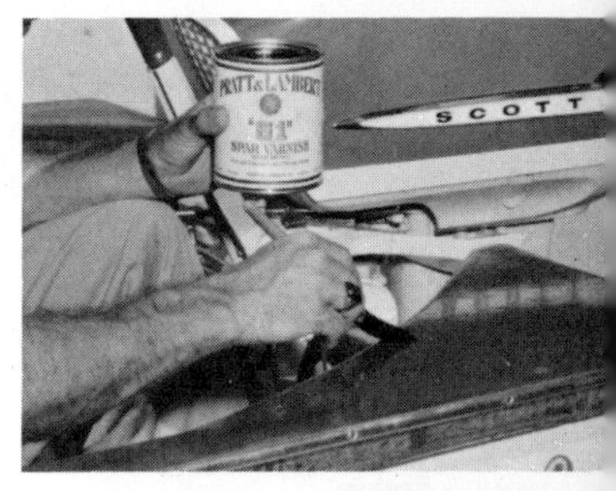

It's easy to keep a boat clean by ple washing. Above: A garden hose and sponge remove the dirt and grime, or salt deposits in salt-water areas. Varnished parts of a hull (upper right) add greatly to a craft's appearance. lowever, care must be taken in applying coats of varnish. To hide dents, cks, and chips, which come from normal boat use, touch up with matching paint (right). Use regular paint and a brush or a spray can to restore the craft's finish

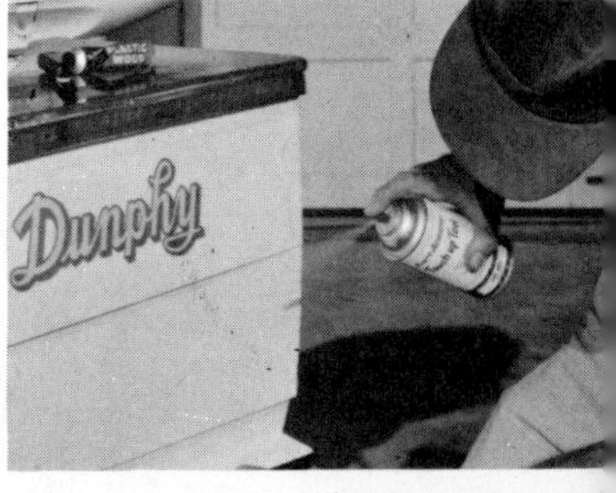

hydrogen peroxide before new coats are applied. When the surface is bare and smooth, clean it off with a rag soaked in turpentine. Avoid heat or strong sunshine when painting, also high humidity and rainy days. Keep the paint well stirred and clean the brushes between coats. Make the first, or primer, coat a thin one and spread with fore and aft strokes, following the grain of the wood. After the first coat has dried thoroughly, sand the hull lightly. Then apply the second and third coats. The next year, the surface can be sanded lightly, cleaned with turpentine, and brought back to beauty with one new coat.

With fiberglass hulls, do not use the standard oil-base paints. Instead try one of the new two-component

Look for harmony in choosing colors

epoxy-base paints over a special primer. Epoxy has a chemical affinity for fiberglass and adheres by a chemical-mechanical bond, resulting in a very hard, smooth surface. Raw aluminum is best painted by first removing all the grease with a non-oil solvent, next applying a special primer coat, then finishing with a hard vinyl paint.

The techniques for varnishing are much the same, except varnish should never be stirred. This will merely permit entrance of bubbles into the clear liquid. Brushes must be absolutely clean (new ones are preferred) and the surface free of dust. Never use turpentine in or around varnish work. Varnish sets so fast that attempts to patch up spots will make a mess.

Anti-fouling bottom paint combats marine growth

WINTER STORAGE

Storage requires good hull support

There are three choices for storing a boat between seasons, each with advantages and disadvantages. Indoor storage, at a shipyard or in a garage at home, will best protect the hull from the ravages of winter. Outdoor storage costs less but requires more preparation. Wet storage–securing the boat to a slip–is good for the hull, provided natural hazards can be avoided. Ice is the worst problem. It can cut the planking with the sharpness of a razor blade and the force of a heavy press. Wet storage must be ice free, whether in salt or fresh water. It is a good idea to pull the boat out and paint the bottom before a winter afloat as protection against salt-water barnacles or, in southern waters, the teredo – the marine boring

Canvas cockpit covers must permit some ventilation of the hull

worm. The advantage of wet storage is that the wooden hull will have no chance to dry out and open its seams.

Smaller boats can be kept at home on the trailer, preferably in the garage if there is room. Trailer storage is not ideal. It requires additional bracing along the hull and the roller bearings will need rotation so they don't flatten on one side. Shipyard storage, whether indoors or out, requires a strong, well-supported cradle in which the boat can rest. If outdoors, the boat will need a tarpaulin fitted over it like a tent, so that the rain will run off the canvas. The tarp must be securely tied down and supported from underneath by a wooden framework. Again, the choice is do-it-yourself or pay the shipyard.

WINTER STORAGE

Shipyard storage fees are based on a cost of a couple of dollars or more for each foot of the boat's length. When a boat is being laid up for the winter, it should be thoroughly cleaned, inside and out. The tools are soap and water—even a vacuum cleaner. And the boat must end up bone dry. All combustible materials, such as oily rags, must be removed. Shipyard fires are outright disasters. If a tarpaulin is to be fitted over the boat, ventilation must be provided. Dampness breeds dry rot in the planking.

Outboard runabouts under 18 feet are easily stored by turning them upside down. The interior is thus protected and a tarp, plastic sheeting, or building paper will serve as a cover for the topsides and bottom.

Open storage demands a good cover (left). One owner forgot and snow lies deep in his cockpit. Ice is the enemy when boats are wet stored during winter months

A boat that is inverted and blocked up on either end forms a bridge. Strains will develop and warp the hull unless supplementary blocking is added at a few spots around the gunwales.

A check of the boat in storage is worthwhile from time to time during the off-season. Is the hull support firm? Has the tarp blown off? Do the metal surfaces need another film of oil to discourage rust? Many a skipper enjoys the puttering-around phases of boating during the inactive months. Small repair jobs—installation of a new feature, such as a bait box or a hardware gadget, painting or varnishing of seats or floor boards—these make the time fly. Moreover, boatyards can be great conversation centers.

When cruising, figure fresh water consumption at about two quarts per person per day for cooking and drinking purposes.

When buying an outboard boat, give careful consideration to models with the high, 20-inch transom rather than the 15's. The higher transom is necessary on larger boats, desirable on many smaller ones, although it requires the long-shaft motor. High transoms keep water out of the outboard well and the cockpit.

Don't drill holes indiscriminately in fiberglass hulls when mounting hardware. Check with a dealer to determine the safest places for bolts or screws. Many hulls have double bottoms for flotation, the surfaces being separated by air spaces, foam plastic, or balsa wood. These should be kept watertight.

Too many skippers forget to replace the transom drain plugs before launching their boats. Place a sign, "Check Drain Plug," on the trailer winch or boat transom as a reminder.

To protect flooring from stains and scratches, use rubber auto mats under fishing-tackle boxes, fuel tanks, and anchors. Cut fish bait on one of these floor mats.

If the boat is used in salt water, wipe salt spray off exposed metal parts, especially an outboard motor, with a clean rag and spread on a light film of oil. This will stop corrosion of metal surfaces exposed to the salt air. If fresh water is available, wash down the decks and topsides.

Don't substitute clothesline, metal chain, or other materials for the tiller cable. They may not be strong enough, may not flex properly, or may stretch and shrink as atmospheric conditions change. Since the steering system is the heart of the boat, use only the best materials.

Clean plastic windshields with plain soap and water. Don't use abrasive powders which will scratch the plastic, or chemical cleaners which may stain it.

From time to time, clean the outboard fuel tanks. Empty the tanks, pour in two ounces of commercial alcohol, slosh it around, and drain. A soft cloth on the end of a stick, will help with interior cleaning. Check the gasket, the priming bulb, and fuel line for signs of wear.

The Coast Guard maintains a continuous listening watch over 2,182 kilocycles on the marine radiotelephone system. This channel is the one to use for emergency distress calls. The Citizens' Band system has no distress channel.

When buying a boat for use in waters with many shoals and sand bars, choose a light, broad-beamed hull to keep draft at a minimum. Flat hulls draw the least water.

Overloading is a common cause of boating fatalities. To determine maximum safe loads in pounds, use this formula: $L \times B \times D \times \frac{0.6}{12} \times 150$, where $L =$ length, $B =$ beam, and $D =$ depth. Besides the formula, when a boat feels or looks overloaded, it probably is.

STARCRAFT
WS-1128-DD